Oyster Plates

Jim and Vivian Karsnitz

Schiffer Publishing Ltd

77 Lower Valley Road, Atglen, PA 19310

DEDICATED
TO
Tristan, Ross, Michael and Patrick
Kathi and Craig
Barb and Jim

Printed in the United States of America.
ISBN: 0-88740-529-0

Published by Schiffer Publishing, Ltd.
77 Lower Valley Road
Atglen, PA 19310
Please write for a free catalog.
This book may be purchased from the publisher.
Please include $2.95 postage.
Try your bookstore first.

We are interested in hearing from authors
with book ideas on related subjects.

Acknowledgements

In acquiring material for this book, we have become indebted to dozens of people. Some opened up their collections to photography and others opened up their minds, providing us with new information. The result of many years of collecting and experience, they gave freely of their special resources. It would be impossible to list everyone and we hesitate to list any, because we must then draw a line. There were however, a few who provided valuable information and went the extra mile in accommodating our questions. The staff of the Thomas A. Edison Winter Home, Mary D. Harris, Bill Hodnick, Evelyn Jones, Harry and Hebe Marsh, Dave Mink, Rudy and Roberta Schmehl, Betty Schulz, John and Louise Winters and Thomas M. Woodward all provided material on oyster plates and silverware. Michael Murphy, Harold Reist and Diona M. Snively gave us technical assistance. Our thanks for permission to photograph her collection goes to Betty Griswold. To each we are grateful, for their help has made this effort even more valuable for the readers.

Foreword

As our enthusiasm for hunting decoys and sporting antiques led us into this field of more specialized interest in oysters, this book project grew into much more than we originally planned. The oyster cans and tools of the oyster trade are used by some decoy collectors as "go withs," spicing up the display of their collections, and this is what we intended to document when we began this research. As we compiled the information, we learned much more about oysters and the items associated with them. The plates, silverware and other items used to serve oysters and the Victorian flair with which they were eaten captivated us. The period when oysters were most popular was known for its opulance. A variety of styles of many unusual items were created for and used with oysters.

We have always enjoyed eating oysters in all the varied methods of their preparation. As we learned more about the industry and its associated objects, we grew to appreciate the oyster even more. Hopefully, the readers also will gain some of our enthusiasm. This is another fascinating area for extended research and collecting pleasure. We invite correspondence on the subject, addressed through the publisher, and look forward to future contacts with kindred souls.

A companion volume, *Oyster Cans*, by the authors, presents the story of the oyster from the shucking house to the consumer. Here is a treasury of over 800 different oyster cans, shucking house tools, shipping containers and advertising materials all shown through color photography and identifying text.

Contents

Values

The value of an item is always a subjective judgment. While most people want to know the values of their possessions, finding an accurate number is often elusive. The quoted figure reflects the judgment of the writer and is not necessarily a market consensus. Also, over time, all values are rendered obsolete.

In light of these problems, the authors have chosen to use a rarity system of rating the items. If the reader feels the need for monetary values, a price range can be assigned to each degree of rarity. The result will be as close to reality as any other way of determining value, and the assigned values can be adjusted for new market conditions.

Each item in this book must have different values.

The item's condition is a key to its value, as damaged, repaired or other imperfections seriously affect price. Where only a few like items are available, or for one-of-a-kind items, the values are widely variable.

In this book, the following rarity designations apply:
* COMMON
** SCARCE
*** RARE
**** VERY RARE
*****ONLY A FEW KNOWN OR ONE OF A KIND

The captions accompanying the pictures of the plates will list the name of the manufacturer and the plate size, if available.

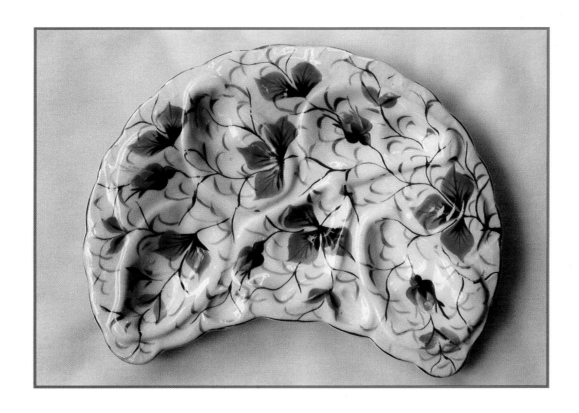

CHAPTER ONE
The Oyster In History

The first person who tasted a raw oyster, because of either hunger or an inquisitive nature, must have been a hardy soul.

The man had sure a palate covered O'er With brass or steel that on the rocky shore First broke the oozy oyster's pearly coat And risked the living morsel down his throat.
John Gay, **Trivia**, 1716 Part III

There is another legend about how the oyster was tasted for the first time. An early man, walking along the shore, noticed some oysters, with their shells open, feeding. Being curious, he picked one up and it immediately snapped shut, pinching his finger. He pulled the finger loose and instinctively put it into his mouth. The result was the first taste of the delicious oyster liquor. The flavor was superb so he picked up the oyster, forced it open, and ate the oyster, beginning man's love affair with the bivalve.

Chinese people and native Americans ate oysters over three thousand years ago and left large shell mounds scattered along the coast wherever oysters were found. The ancient Romans learned to cultivate oysters to be eaten in their legendary feasts. When they conquered England, the Romans found more oysters and arranged transport for them back to Rome. Later, French and English food connoisseurs were equally attracted to the bivalve and devised many ways both to grow and to eat them. Cassanova ate a plate of oysters before his amorous adventures, which gave credence to the legend that oysters have aphrodesiac qualities. Oysters are part of the literature in many countries, as in Shakespeare's **Merry Wives of Windsor,** Act II, Scene II, when Pistol says,
Why then the World's mine Oyster Which I with sword will open.

Labadist missionaries in Brooklyn, New york reported in 1697 that they found oysters "large and full, some a foot long."[1] The historian Strachey, in

The Very First Oyster Eaten-**
At First Fright, Then Delight
Harper's Weekly October, 1879

Historie of Travaile into Virginia Britannia, said he saw oysters thirteen inches long.

Oysters gained popularity as a culinary delicacy through the ages until their zenith during the late Victorian era, indeed the nineteenth century is sometimes called the Oyster Century. Oysters were served not only to gourmets in lavish style at city restaurants, but every town also had its own saloon, bar or "hotel" featuring oysters. Almost every such establishment had the word "oyster" in its name and even cities of modest size had dozens of oyster houses. Only because of a declining supply and corresponding

Victorian Oyster Bar**

Opening of the Oyster Season**
Harper's Weekly September, 1882

increase in price, coupled with a change in fashion at the end of the Victorian age, did oysters go out of favor. Today, oysters enjoy a modest increase in popularity, especially at gourmet oyster bars, but nothing to compare with their hayday after the Civil War until the early 1900s.

In America, in the late nineteenth century, it became fashionable to eat oysters in large quantities, so that one or two hundred were not considered excessive.

New York City was the destination of a great number of oysters because of its large market, but the sale of oysters was similar in many cities and towns, only on a smaller scale. New York oyster cellars, where oysters were served to the public, were usually basements of homes and rather plain on the outside, but very fancy inside. They became gathering places for politicians and the social elite, somewhat like coffee houses in Europe. Downing's, at Number 5 Broad Street, was a leading New York establishment. Here all sorts of politics, art and philosophy was discussed amid damask tablecloths, silver service and crystal chandeliers.[2]

The "Canal Street plan," as popular at the establishments on Canal Street as elsewhere, was developed whereby the customer was served all the oysters he could eat for the price of six pence. The establishment seldom lost money on this seemingly generous arrangement since a bad oyster would be slipped on the plate of a greedy customer, usually ending his desire for more. In addition to oyster cellars, oyster peddlers circulated throughout the city selling from pushcarts.[3]

[01] Kochiss, John, **"Oystering from New York to Boston"** Wesylan Univ. Press, 1974

[02] ibid.

[03] ibid.

Southern Oyster Peddler**
Harper's Weekly March. 1889

Oyster Girl**

Peddlers Oyster Pail***
Ronald L. Newcomb Collection

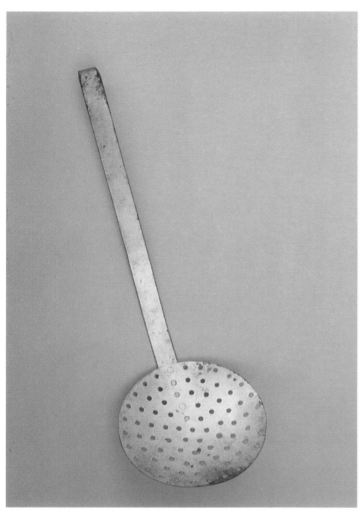

Peddlers Oyster Ladle**

Peddlers Oyster Pail***
Ronald L. Newcomb Collection

Raking in Shallow Water**
Harper's Weekly January, 1890

Working the Beds off Annapolis**
Harper's Weekly January, 1890

Many oysters sold in New York City came from the two-story oyster barges anchored in the East River along East Street. Sailing vessels brought fresh oysters to the water side and unloaded them onto the decks of the barges where they were sorted, barrelled, and loaded onto wagons or peddlers' carts at the street side for delivery throughout the city. An office was located on the first floor of the barge while the second floor served as storage for barrels and other equipment.

Just as specialized tableware was developed for eating oysters, suppliers of cooking equipment provided many distinctive items to prepare oysters. The catalog of V. Clad & Sons of Philadelphia lists specialty tools. Steam or gas fired oyster stewers, oyster steamers, stew pans, broilers and chafing dishes were available. They were used in commercial oyster houses and private homes alike, for cooking oysters in the varied styles that people grew to expect.

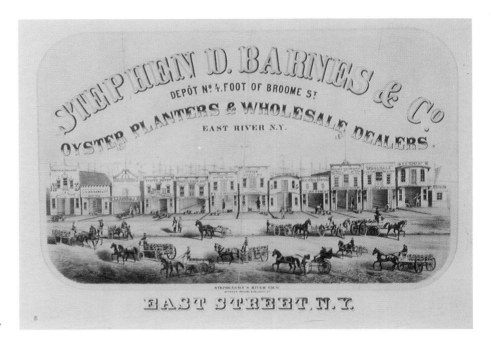

Oyster Barges On East Street**

By the mid-1820s, a growing demand throughout the country and improved transportation caused the supply of oysters to be exhausted in the beds around New York City, Long Island and northern New Jersey. Oyster boats moved north to New England and south to the Delaware River and Chesapeake Bay. At first, wild oysters were gathered, but as they diminished cultivated beds were established and many laws were enacted to control the natural and cultivated beds and their harvests. "Oyster Wars" were fought where men were killed and injured, and fortunes were made and lost, over the control of this important resource, known as "sunken treasure." Today, many watermen consider the oyster a God-given crop to be harvested by those strong enough to do so. Oysters are planted and harvested, much as dirt farmers plant and harvest their crops. Today in Maryland, the "hunter-gatherer" method of harvest continues. With increased population and natural diseases, it appears that the days of the independent harvester are numbered unless attitudes are changed.

Catalog, V. Clad & Sons***
Philadelphia, PA

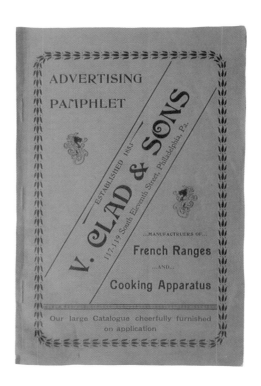

Catalog, V. Clad & Sons***
Philadelphia, PA

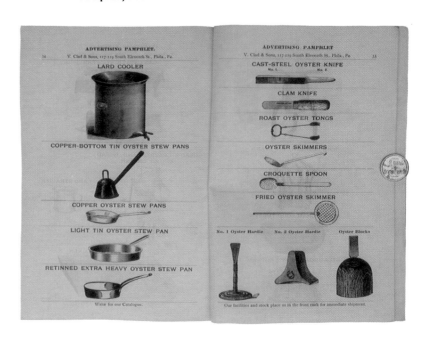

Oyster Processing Tools***

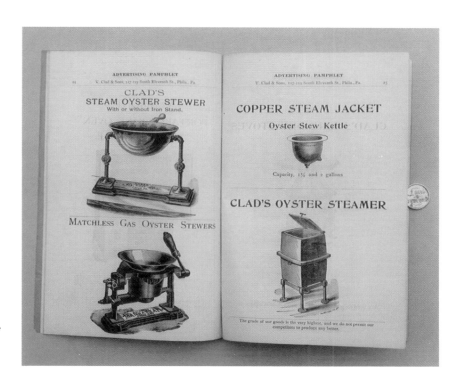

Oyster Stewers and Steamers***

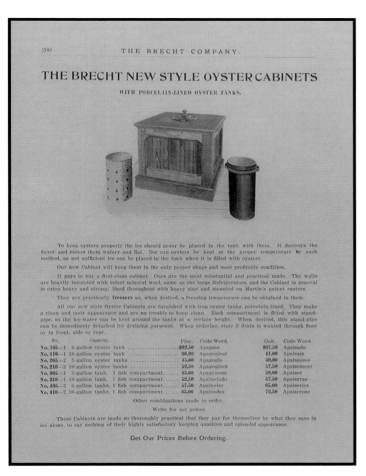

Brecht Oyster Cabinets***
Joe Secrist Collection

Brecht Oyster Cabinets***
Joe Secrist Collection

The American eating oyster, *Crassostrea Virginica*, is found along the East Coast of North America and west to Texas. It is different from oysters found on the west coast of America, in Europe or the Orient in that the pearl is inferior in this oyster; the true pearl here is the oyster itself. The American oyster differs greatly in size and flavor depending on where it is grown. Each area has its peculiar environmental factors that make its oysters different. Connoisseurs contend they can determine where the oysters grew by the subtile changes in color and taste that the location of the beds bring to the oyster, and they use terms to describe the taste that are reminiscent of those used by wine lovers. Oysters are described as salty and tangy with a hickory flavor, or mild and creamy smooth, and many other wine-associated adjectives. In addition, certain varieties are prescribed as best for each recipe. People in each geographical area honestly believe their oysters are the best. Blue Points from Long Island, Toms Cove Oysters from Chincoteague, Virginia, and seaside vs. bayside oysters each have their following. It is easy to start an argument over the merits of each, such as whether they are better salty from the ocean or milder from the bay.

On the Pacific Coast, the Olympic oyster, *Ostrea Lurida*, is native and much smaller than its Atlantic coast relative, although no less flavorful. European and Asiatic oysters are grown commercially on both coasts under controlled conditions. Thus, a gourmet oyster bar today serves many varieties and local variations. Deciding which variety to order is, like choosing a fine wine, an educated skill.

While oysters are edible at any time, tradition and conservation have limited most oyster eating to the months whose names include the letter "r," September through April. Many people believe this tradition

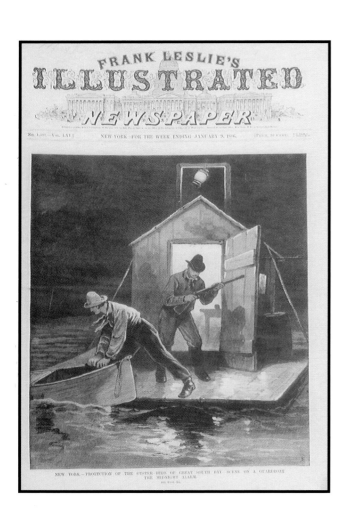

New York-Protection of the Oyster-Beds**
of Great South Bay-Scene on a Guard Boat, the Midnight Alarm
Leslie's Illustrated January, 1886

The Oyster War in Chesapeake Bay**
Harper's Weekly March, 1884

14

AN ENGAGEMENT IN THE OYSTER WAR ON THE CHESAPEAKE.—FROM A SKETCH BY F. CRESSON SCHELL.—[SEE PAGE 23.]

An Engagement in the Oyster War on**
the Chesapeake
Harper's Weekly January, 1886

developed to avoid spoilage during hot weather, and while this was true to some extent when refrigeration was not available, another equally valid reason exists. Oysters naturally spawn in the spring and summer and therefore are thin and have poor flavor if harvested from the wild at that stage. Since spawning is necessary to ensure a continuing supply, the laws prohibiting harvesting in the summer may protect the oyster even more than people. Farmed oyster beds, where conditions are more controlled, can ensure a continuous supply of many varieties.

CHAPTER TWO

Oyster Plates and Serving Pieces

The numerous items linked to the oyster industry can provide a pleasant interest for many people. Those who made a show of a meal in the late 19th century required special service pieces for each item on the menu. Oyster plates were made in an endless parade of designs and colors, the fancier the better. Also, silver serving utensils complemented the plates, and together they are searched for today. Shown in this Chapter are over four hundred oyster plates.

While oysters have been eaten since ancient times, the people of the Victorian age brought their serving to its highest degree of opulance. In America in the late nineteenth century, as fortunes were made, people began to travel extensively. They saw oyster related items of china and silver in the grand hotels, dining cars and steamships and had to have them in their own homes. Formal dinners of five to eighteen courses were not unusual, and a rigid etiquette dictated a different service for each course, bringing oyster plates and silver serving utensils into popularity. This style of living continued until the start of World War I.

Oysters were plentiful at the turn of the twentieth century and were eaten in large quantities. A dozen raw oysters were merely the starting point, and many people would eat six dozen or more and then continue on to a full course meal. Legend has it that Diamond Jim Brady would eat well over one hundred raw oysters at Delmonico's Restaurant in New York City before proceeding with the rest of his meal.

Table Setting

Within the shell of some oysters lives a small crab, called the oyster crab, which shares the space as well as the food. Some people consider them a delicacy, and when oysters were eaten in large quantities enough were found to prepare a special dish. The crabs also were added to oyster stews to enrich them. An oyster crab is modeled into one of the wells of the Etruscan majolica plate.

A poem written about the oyster (from Chapter IV of Lewis Carroll's *Through the Looking Glass,* 1871, entitled "The Walrus and the Carpenter") finishes by indicating the oyster's popularity:

"O oysters," said the Carpenter, "You've had a pleasant run! Shall we be trotting home again?" But answer came there none-And this was scarcely odd, because They'd eaten every one.

The Victorian hostesses who served oysters in their diningrooms wanted their service to be as delicate as possible. Several types of dishes were developed to accommodate this need.

One style, developed to serve oysters in the half shell on ice, had a deep-welled plate developed for this. Today we might identify this plate as a soup bowl because of its depth, but the inside rim is scalloped where oysters were to be placed on ice. An underplate was used with this dish to catch any melted ice that overflowed. The plates for use with ice are not nearly as collectible as are the ones that were developed to hold oysters removed from their shells. Some people today call these "oyster stew" plates, and they may well have been used for this purpose also.

Etruscan Majolica★★★★★
Griffin, Smith & Hill Phoenixville, PA Rare Oyster Plate Note Oyster Crab in Bottom Well 9 ⅞ inches
Collection of John Boraten, Sr.

Oysters served on ice on the Half-Shell
Dockside Seafood

A second type of plate was designed to serve oysters on the half-shell without ice. These probably pleased hostesses since there was no ice to contend with. This type had larger, less sharply-defined wells into which the shell could be placed. These plates also can be identified as "oyster plates," but they lack the ornate design generally associated with that term. This style provided a compromise for the hostess's desire for neatness and the gourmand's wish for the oyster liquor with the meat. A gourmand also would prefer to have ice to keep the oysters very cold. The hostess could accommodate this by removing the oysters from ice to the plate immediately before serving. A problem associated with this style was the rough oyster shell scratching the plate.

Oysters served on the Half-Shell
Dockside Seafood

A third style of plate, most often seen today, has recesses for the oyster without its shell and without ice. It is very ornate in many designs, most with wells that look like oyster shells. The hostess was pleased with this style because it was not prone to scratches and did not accommodate the messy ice.

Plates of all three styles were made and used throughout the period. Nearly all oyster plates collected today were made in the period 1860 to 1910, or from about the end of the Civil War to the beginning of World War I.

Oysters served on Oyster Plate Without Shell
Dockside Seafood

True oyster aficionados still frequent oyster bars or saloons scattered around the world for fresh oysters served very cold on the half shell over ice. They pick up the oyster and tip the shell to the lips, taking both the liquor and oyster into their mouth, saying this is the only way to really enjoy oysters. Some may squeeze the juice from a quarter lemon to flavor the oysters and feel that any other sauce spoils the true flavor. Classic oyster saloons wrapped the lemon in cheese-cloth to prevent the seeds from falling on the oyster.

To supply oyster plates to the growing Victorian market, companies in the United States and Europe made varieties in porcelain, majolica pottery, glass, silver and pewter. The plate designers, in their efforts to create something different, used many kinds of shellfish and sea life in the decorations.

Clam shells were often used for wells, and some collectors call these clam plates, but during Victorian times clams were not as popular as oysters. Additionaly, unlike oysters, clams toughen as they become older and larger so raw clams large enough to fill the wells would not be edible. It seems doubtful that these plates were made to contain clams. Dave Mink, of the Sansom Street Oyster House in Philadelphia, has put forth a theory that the early plates made in Europe had the oyster found on the Brittany coast of France as a model for their wells. The French oyster, called the Belon after the Belon River in Finiste're, was considered superior to other European oysters. The shape of the Belon is rounded, not elongated like the American oyster. If the well was modeled after the Belon, it could easily have been mistaken for a clam shell by Americans. The shape of the well can help to date oyster plates.

Longchamp***
13 ¾ inches
Courtesy of Hebe's Antiques

Longchamp***
13 inches
Courtesy of Hebe's Antiques

Longchamp***
8 inches
Courtesy of Hebe's Antiques

Longchamp★★★
9 ⅜ inches
Courtesy of Hebe's Antiques

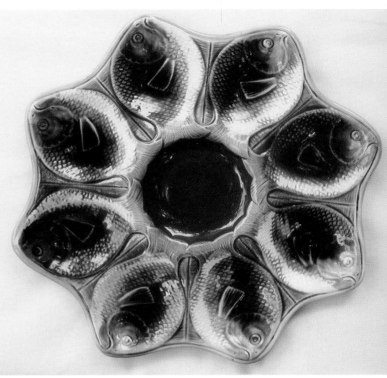

Unmarked★★★
10 ⅝
Courtesy of Hebe's Antiques

France DV★★★
12 inches
Courtesy of Evelyn Jones Antiques

Chantilly, France★★★
13 inches
Courtesy of Evelyn Jones Antiques

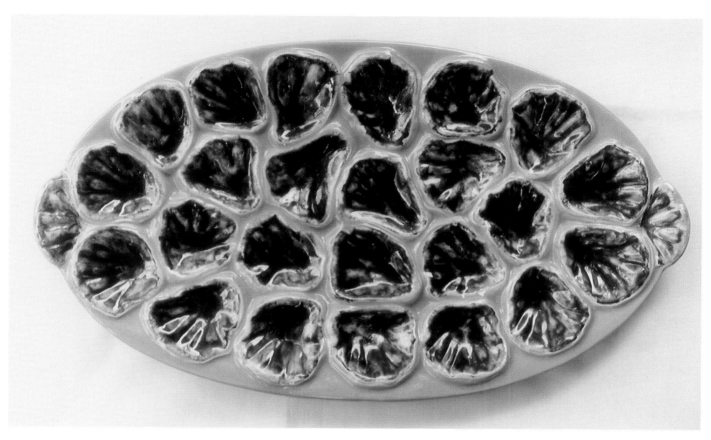

France, Bivent****
24 Oyster Platter 21 ⅞ inches by 12 ¾ inches
Courtesy of Hebe's Antiques

Quimper***
Ross Marie #9 '68 13 inches
Courtesy of Fisherman's Inn

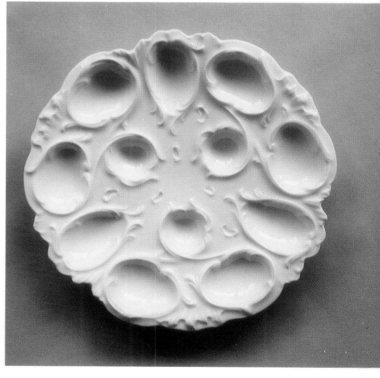

Limoges, France**
Undecorated 9 ½ inches
Courtesy of Fisherman's Inn

Lanternier,***
Limoges, France Handled Plate 9 ⅝ inches
Courtesy of Hebe's Antiques
2/13 R57-17

Charles Martin, Limoges, France***
Palace de Cristal Marche aux Herbes, Bruxelles 16 oyster platter
with dolphin handle 12 inches
Courtesy of Hebe's Antiques

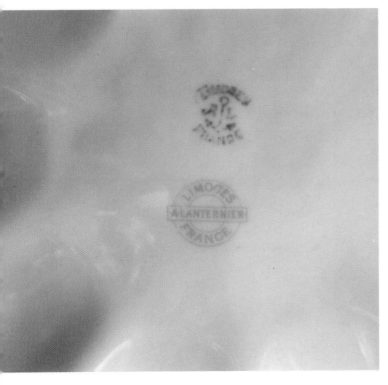

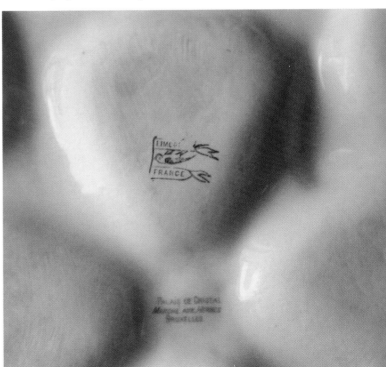

Logo for Above

Logo for above

The number of depressions to contain oysters in plates seems to be an arbitrary point. These "wells," as they are called, range from one to six, with two wells being very rare. In addition, larger plates and platters were made to hold one or two dozen oysters, and even a three tiered, lazy susan was made by Minton for twenty-seven oysters. Additional small spaces in the plates were used for a sauce or lemons. Some plates have larger additional spaces and these could have been used to serve oyster crackers.

Oyster plate design patents have been issued in the United States since 1874. Some of these patent designs actually can be found on plates; however, it is probable that not all of them reached production.

Minton, Special Order*****
Lazy Susan for 27 oysters Three entwined fish finial 10 inches by 12 inches
Courtesy of Hebe's Antiques

Close Up of Finials

Moser Glass Co.****
8 ⅛ inches
Courtesy of Hebe's Antiques

Moser Glass Co.****
7 ¾ inches
Courtesy of Hebe's Antiques

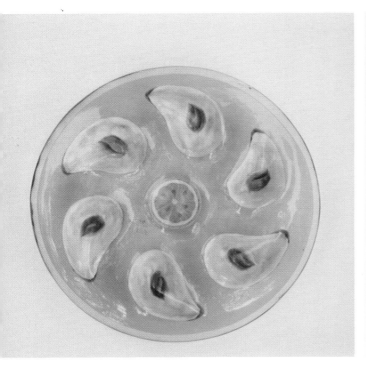

Moser Glass Co.****
8 ⅛ inches
Courtesy of Hebe's Antiques

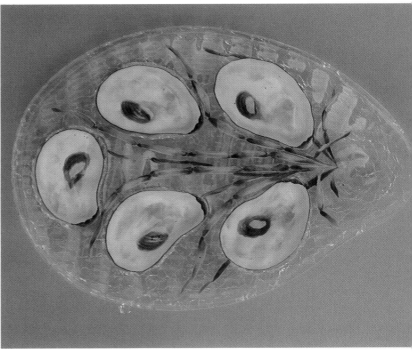

Moser Glass Co.****
7 ¼ inches
Courtesy of Hebe's Antiques

Moser Glass Co.****
7 ¼ inches
Courtesy of Hebe's Antiques

Etruscan Majolica*****
Griffin, Smith & Hill Phoenixville, PA 9 ⅞ inches
Collection of John Boraten, Sr.

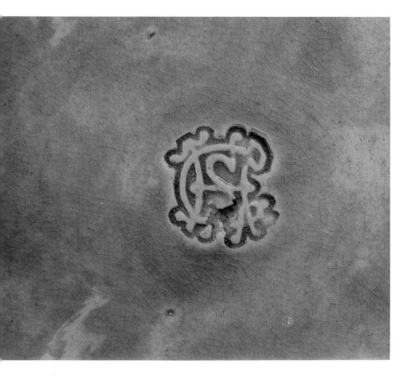

Logo for Griffin, Smith & Hill

Underside of Plate

Sabino,★★★★
Paris, France 7 ⅞ Inches
Courtesy of Hebe's Antiques

Logo For Above

Union Porcelain Works***
Greenpoint, NY 8 ½ inches by 6 1/4 inches
Courtesy of Hebe's Antiques

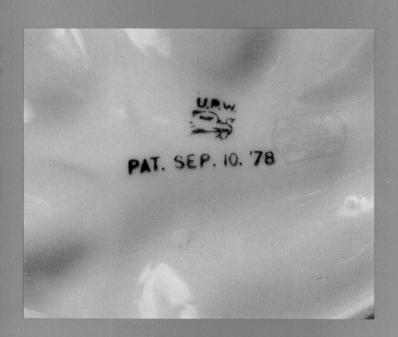

Union Porcelain Works***
Greenpoint, NY 9 ¼ inches
Courtesy of Hebe's Antiques

Union Porcelain Works***
Greenpoint, NY 10 ¼ inches by 7 ¾ inches
Courtesy of Hebe's Antiques

Union Porcelain Works***
Greenpoint, NY 8 ½ inches by 6 ¼ inches
Courtesy of Hebe's Antiques

Union Porcelain Works***
Greenpoint, NY 10 ¼ inches by 7 ¾ inches
Courtesy of Hebe's Antiques

Union Porcelain Works***
Greenpoint, NY 10 ¼ inches
Courtesy of Hebe's Antiques

Union Porcelain Works***
Greenpoint, NY 8 ¾ inches by 5 ½ inches
Courtesy of Hebe's Antiques

Sterling Silver***
9 ½ inches
Courtesy of Fisherman's Inn

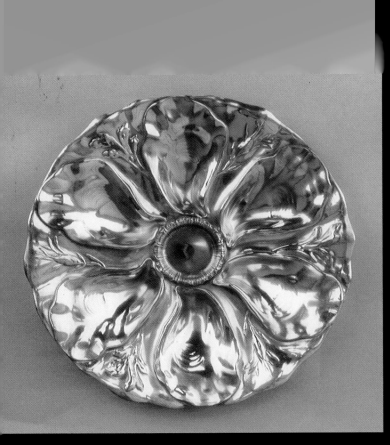

Reed and Barton Sterling Silver***
9 ½ inches
Courtesy of Hebe's Antiques

Pennsylvania Railroad Regular Dining Car Service***
8 ⅜ inches
Courtesy of Oyster and Maritime Museum of Chincoteague Island

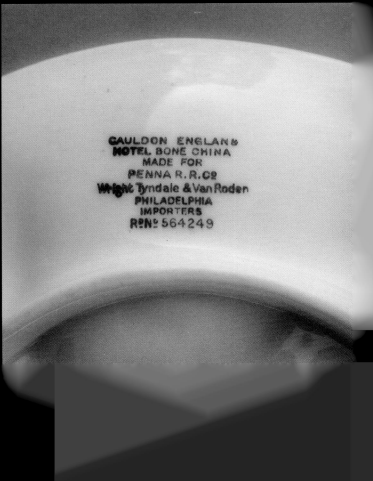

Pennsylvania Railroad Executive Dining Car Service****
8 ⅜ inches
Art Burbage Collection

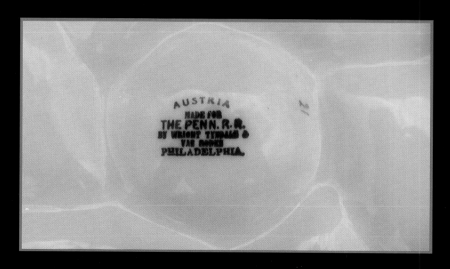

AUSTRIA
MADE FOR
THE PENN. R. R.
BY WRIGHT TYNDALE &
VAN RODEN
PHILADELPHIA.

Logo for above

Many celebrities have had oyster plates made specifically for them, including America's 19th President, Rutherford B. Hayes, who served from 1877 to 1881. He commissioned a state dining service for the White House, including oyster plates designed by Mr. Theodore R. Davis, an artist employed by *Harper's Weekly*. The set was made by the Haviland Company in France. In this design, five wells are surrounded by southern raccoon oysters which have the outsides of the shells showing. These shells form a pattern that resembles the outline of a turkey, so the plates are known as the "turkey oyster plates" to collectors. The plate illustrated was made by Haviland after producing the White House china. The presidential set caused a stir among the public, with strong feelings in support and opposition. Mr. Davis patented his design on August 10, 1880. Because of the great expense incurred in making the White House china, he and Haviland sought to recover their expenses by selling similar sets to the public. These sets have the patent date on the backs while the presidential set does not. It is interesting that when the Presidential set was made, the cost was $3120.00, a figure the Congress felt was excessive.

Haviland & Co.★★★★★
Limoges, France President Rutherford B. Hayes 1880
"Turkey" Oyster Plate 8 ¾ inches
Courtesy of Hebe's Antiques

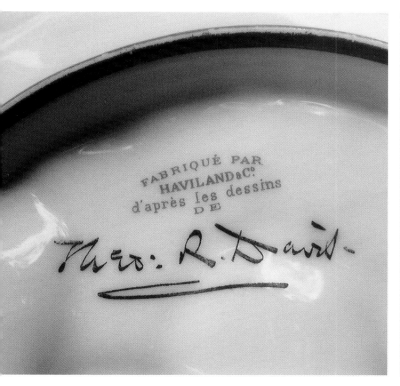

Theo. R. Davis Artist's Signature

Logo for Presidential Oyster Plate Design Patented August 10, 1880

Presidential Seal

Underside of Presidential Plate

Inventor Thomas A. Edison was an owner of a turkey oyster plate made by Haviland for sale to the public. This beautiful set is on display in the dining room of his winter home in Fort Myers, Florida. These plates were sold by Davis, Collamore & Co. of New York City, as indicated on the bottoms of the plates.

Several china stores ordered oyster plates directly from the manufacturers with the store's name printed on the bottoms of the plates along with the name of the maker. Similarly shaped plates were individualized by changing the color or decoration. In some instances, white blanks were imported to be decorated by the retailer. Usually the maker's logo was placed on the plate before it was first fired. When it was decorated later, the decorator's logo is found above the first glaze and can be recognized by this difference.

Thomas A. Edison***
"Turkey" Oyster Plate Haviland & Co., Limoges, France Made for Davis, Collamore, New York 8 ¾ inches

Greenwood China***
Trenton, NJ Maryland State Seal 8 ⅞ inches
Courtesy of Fisherman's Inn

Logo for Above Large Black Numbers is Museum Accession Information

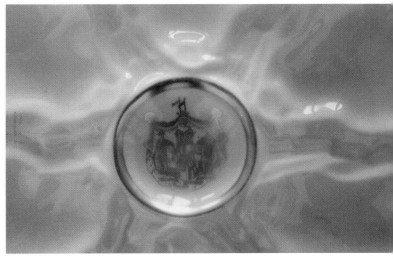

Close-up of Maryland State Seal

In an 1899 Higgins and Seiter catalog, a full page advertisement for Limoges and Weimar oyster plates lists the prices between $4.00 and $24.00 per dozen.

Quimper, France***
HB Quimper 9 ⅛ inches
Courtesy of Fisherman's Inn

Quimper, France***
9 ⅞ inches
Courtesy of Fisherman's Inn

Quimper, France***
HB Quimper Early Fish Design 10 inches
Courtesy Fisherman's Inn

Quimper, France***
9 ⅞ inches
Courtesy of Hebe's Antiques

Quimper, France***
9 ⅞ inches
Courtesy of Hebe's Antiques

Quimper, France***
9 ¼ inches
Courtesy of Evelyn Jones Antiques

Quimper, France***
HR Henriot 9 ½ inches
Courtesy of Hebe's Antiques

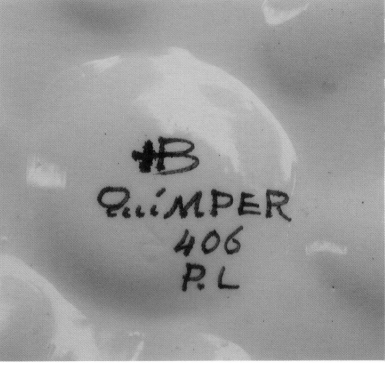

Logo for above

Quimper, France***
8 ¾ inches
Courtesy of Hebe's Antiques

Quimper, France***
HB Quimper 9 inches
Courtesy of Fisherman's Inn

Quimper, France***
Daniel Ross Marie 9 ⅜ inches
Courtesy of Fisherman's Inn

Minton, England****
10 ½ inches

Minton, England****
10 ½ inches
Courtesy of Hebe's Antiques

Minton, England****
10 ½ inches
Courtesy of Hebe's Antiques

Minton, England****
10 ½ inches
Courtesy of Evelyn Jones Antiques

Minton, England****
7 ½ inches by 9 inches
Courtesy Evelyn Jones Antiques

Minton, England****
7 ½ inches by 9 inches
Courtesy of Evelyn Jones Antiques

Minton, England****
7 ½ inches by 9 inches
Courtesy of Hebe's Antiques

Minton, England★★★★
7 ½ inches by 8 ⅞ inches
Courtesy of Hebe's Antiques

Logo for Above Note English Registry Mark

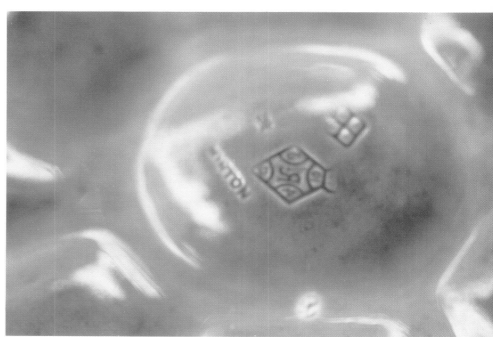

Sarreguemines, France***
Courtesy of Hebe's Antiques

Unmarked Basketweave***
9 ¾ inches
Courtesy of Hebe's Antiques

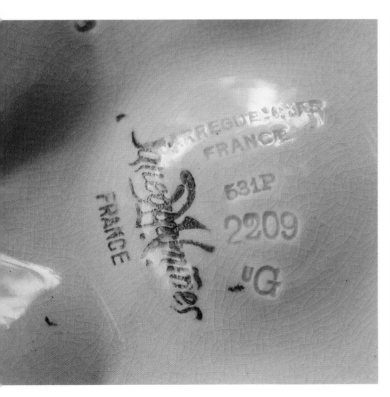

Logo for above

Unmarked Basketweave***
9 ¾ inches
Courtesy Evelyn Jones Antiques

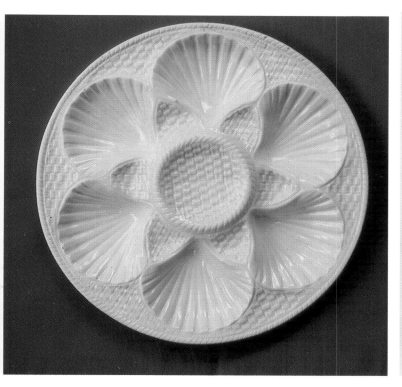

Made in Italy**
12 ⅝ inches
Courtesy of Hebe's Antiques

Wedgwood, England****
9 ⅜ inches
Courtesy of Hebe's Antiques

Unmarked***
Courtesy of Hebe's Antiques

Wedgwood, England****
10 inches
Courtesy of Hebe's Antiques

Unmarked***
10 inches
Courtesy of Hebe's Antiques

Unmarked****
9 ¼ inches
Wengerts Oyster House

Unmarked***
10 inches
Wengert's Oyster House

George Jones, England****
With Raised Figural Shell 10 inches
Courtesy of Hebe's Antiques

OB, France**
9 ⅞ inches
Courtesy of Hebe's Antiques

S. Fielding, England****
9 ⅛
Courtesy of Evelyn Jones Antiques

Unmarked***
9 ¼ inches
Courtesy of Hebe's Antiques

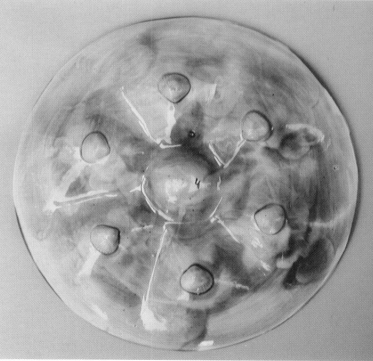

Underside of plate showing seashell feet
Courtesy of Evelyn Jones Antiques

Unmarked***
9 ½ inches
Courtesy of Evelyn Jones Antiques

Longchamp***
8 ⅝ inches
Courtesy of Hebe's Antiques

Unmarked***
9 ¼ inches
Courtesy of Hebe's Antiques

Logo for above

46

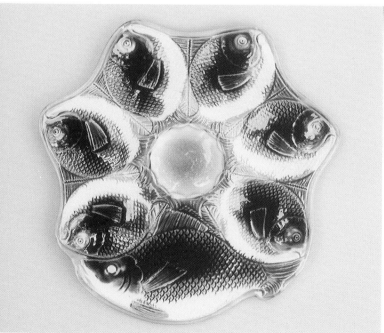

France****
10 ½ inches
Courtesy of Hebe's Antiques

Fishhead with Fish Well for Sauce or Crackers***
9 ¾ inches
Courtesy of Hebe's Antiques

9 ½ inches***
Courtesy of Evelyn Jones Antiques

Sarreguemines, DV France***
10 inches
Courtesy of Evelyn Jones Antiques

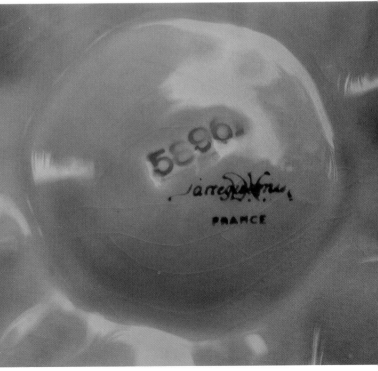

Logo for above

Logo for above

48

Sarreguemines, DV France***
9 ¼ inches
Courtesy of Evelyn Jones Antiques

Unmarked**
10 inches
Courtesy of Fisherman's Inn

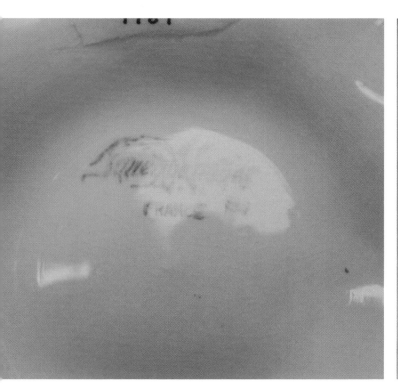

Logo for above

George Jones, England****
8 ⅝ inches
Courtesy of Hebe's Antiques

George Jones, England****
8 ⅝ inches

George Jones, England****
8 ⅝ inches
Courtesy of Hebe's Antiques

50

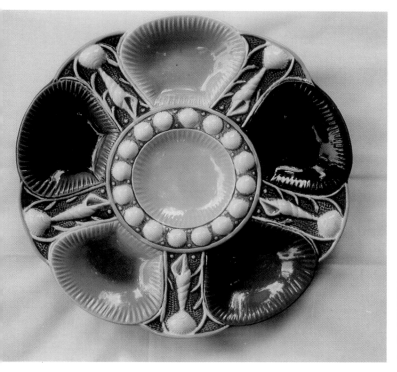

Unmarked***
9 ⅞ inches
Courtesy of Hebe's Antiques

Minton, England****
9 ⅛ inches
Courtesy of Hebe's Antiques

Joseph Holcroft, England 9 ⅞ inches
Courtesy of Hebe's Antiques

Logo of Above

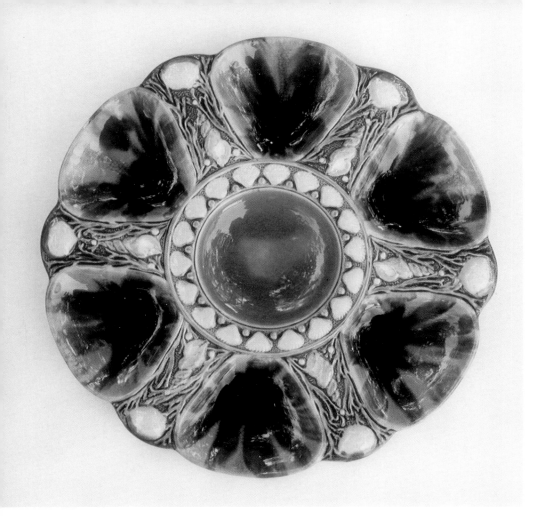

Minton, England****
8 ⅞ inches
Courtesy of Hebe's Antiques

Minton, England****
8 ⅞ inches
Courtesy of Hebe's Antiques

52

Minton, England*****
8 7/8 inches
Courtesy of Hebe's Antiques

Wedgwood, England****
Dolphin dividers 9 1/8 inches
Courtesy of Hebe's Antiques

Wedgwood 1878, England****
9 1/8 inches
Courtesy of Hebe's Antiques

53

Longchamp***
9 ⅜ inches
Courtesy of Evelyn Jones Antiques

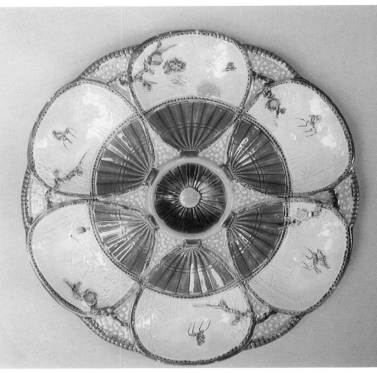

S. Fielding, England*****
9 ½ inches
Courtesy of Evelyn Jones Antiques

Logo for above

Wedgwood, England***
9 ⅜ inches
Courtesy of Evelyn Jones Antiques

Wedgwood, England***
9 ¼ inches
Courtesy of Evelyn Jones Antiques

Minton, England***
9 ¼ inches

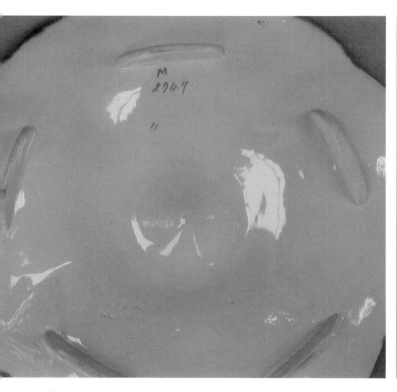

Note Broken Circle Feet for above

Logo for above

Samuel Lear, Hanley, England****
Sunflower, 9 ¾ inches
Courtesy of Evelyn Jones Antiques

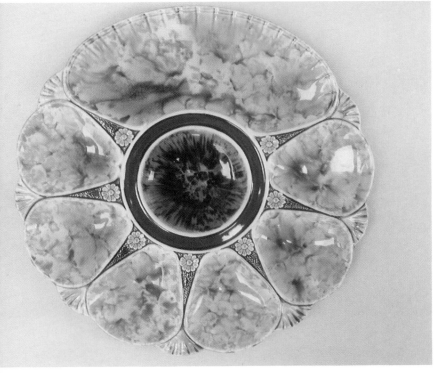

Minton, England***
10 inches
Courtesy of Evelyn Jones Antiques

Minton, England***
10 inches
Courtesy of Evelyn Jones Antiques

Minton, England***
10 inches
Courtesy of Fisherman's Inn

Logo for above

Minton, England***
9 ¼ inches
Courtesy of Hebe's Antiques

Unmarked***
8 ⅛ inches
Courtesy of Hebe's Antiques

Patented by J.W.Boteler, June 16, 1874****
First Design Patent 8 ⅞ inches
Courtesy of Hebe's Antiques

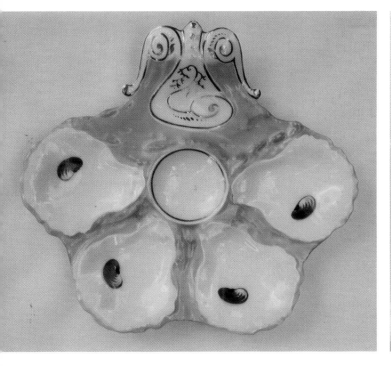

Unmarked***
8 ¾ inches
Courtesy of Hebe's Antiques

Logo for above, See Design Patent Number 7491

Unmarked***
8 ⅞ inches
Courtesy of Hebe's Antiques

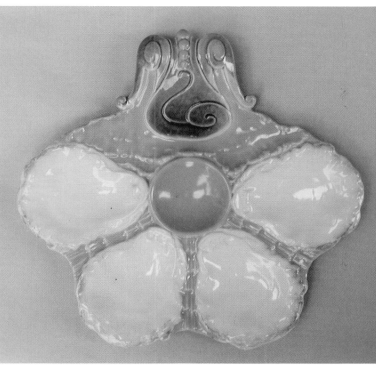

Unmarked***
8 ⅞ inches
Courtesy of Evelyn Jones Antiques

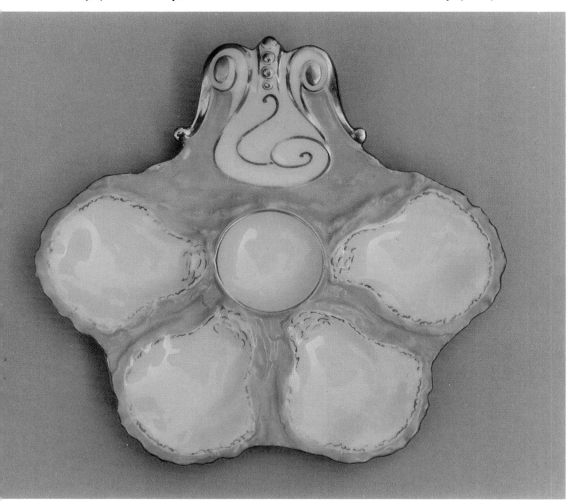

Patented by J.W. Boteler****
June 16, 1874 8 ½ inches
Courtesy of Hebe's Antiques

Patented by J.W.Boteler*****
June 16, 1874 8 ½ inches
Courtesy of Hebe's Antiques

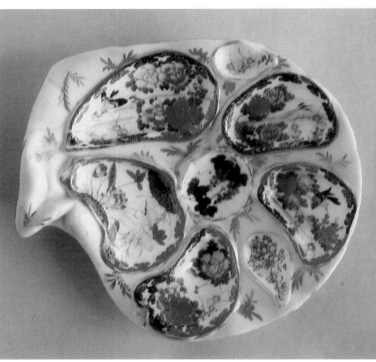

Unmarked***
9 ¼ inches
Courtesy of Fisherman's Inn

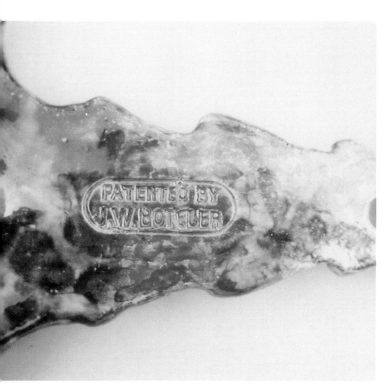

Logo For Above

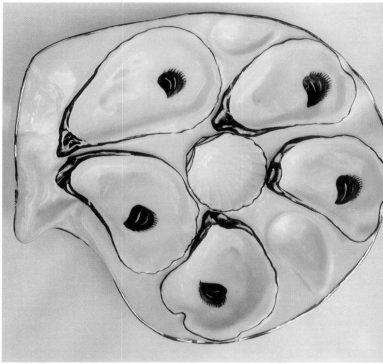

Unmarked***
9 ¼ inches
Courtesy of Hebe's Antiques

Individual Oyster Plates***

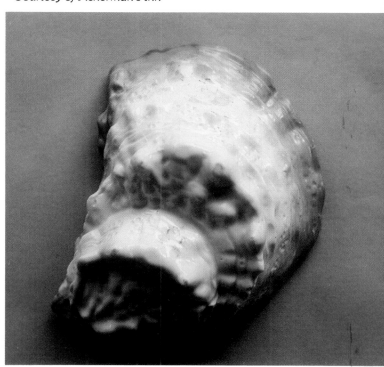

Individual Oyster Plates***
Courtesy of Fisherman's Inn

Individual Oyster Plates***

Reverse of above

Tressemann & Vogt***
Limoges, France Monogrammed Individual Oyster Plates
Mary and Carlton Riggin Collection

G & Co., Royal China Works***
Worcester, England 1 ½ inches, Paper Thin China
Courtesy of Hebe's Antiques

Mark & Gutherz***
Carlsbad 8 ¾ inches
William M. Hodnik Collection

Three Wells

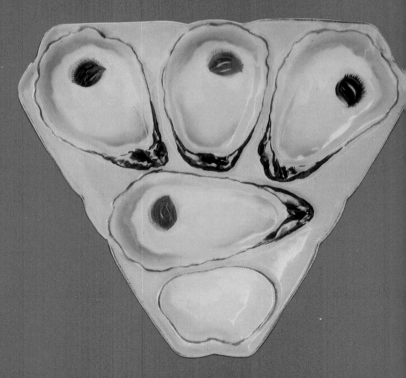

Limoges, France***
6 inches
Courtesy of Hebe's Antiques

Unmarked***
7 inches
Courtesy of Hebe's Antiques

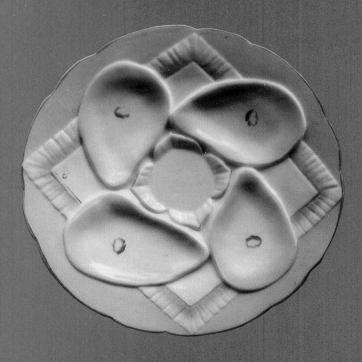

Unmarked**
8 ½ inches
Courtesy Fisherman's Inn

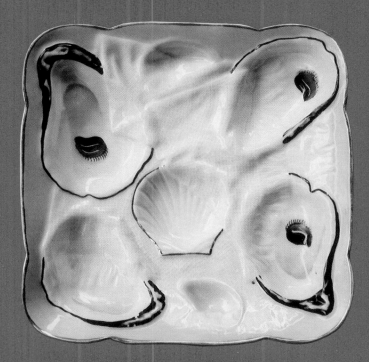

Unmarked***
7 ⅛ inches
Courtesy of Hebe's Antiques

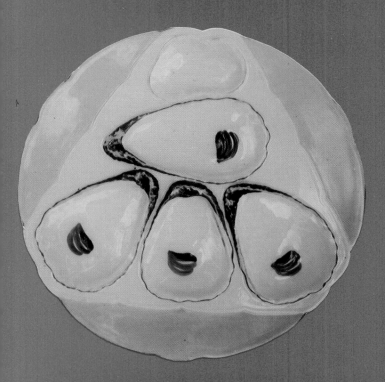

Unmarked***
8 ¼ inches
Courtesy of Hebe's Antiques

Unmarked**
7 inches
Courtesy of Hebe's Antiques

Haviland & Co.***
Limoges, France 7 ¾ inches
Courtesy of Hebe's Antiques

C.& E. Carstens, Porcelain Factory***
Blankenhain, Germany Weimar 8 ¼ inches
Courtesy of Hebe's Antiques

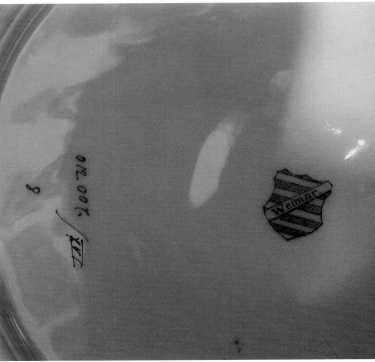

Logo for above

Logo for above

Unmarked**
7 ⅛ inches
Courtesy of Hebe's Antiques

Charles Field Haviland,**
Gerard, Dufraisseix and Morel Limoges, France 7 ½ inches
Courtesy of Hebe's Antiques

M. Redon, France**
American Amateur Decoration, Masonic 7 ½ inches
Courtesy Evelyn Jones Antiques

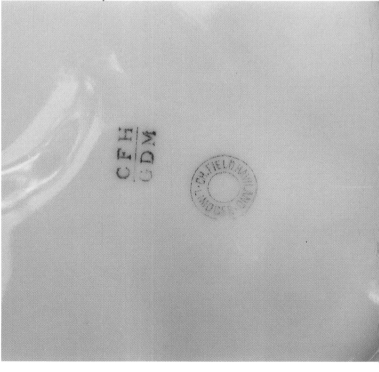

Logo for above

65

Unmarked**
7 ⅛ inches
Courtesy of Hebe's Antiques

Haviland & Co.**
Limoges, France 8 ¾ inches
Courtesy of Hebe's Antiques

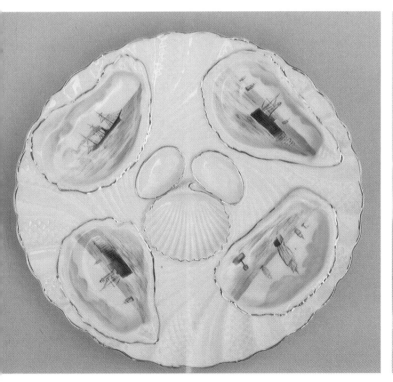

Germany***
8 ½ Inches
Courtesy of Hebe's Antiques

Logo for above

66

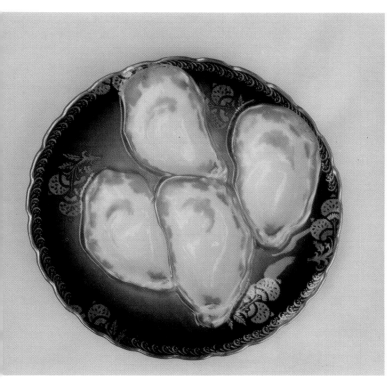

Cobalt Blue, ★★★
7 ⅛ inches
Courtesy of Hebe's Antiques

Haviland & Co.★★★
Limoges, France 7 ⅛ inches
Courtesy of Hebe's Antiques

Tariff Information

Logo for above, Information

Unmarked**
9 ½ inches
Courtesy of Fisherman's Inn

Unmarked**
9 inches
Courtesy Hebe's Antiques

Unmarked**
9 inches
Courtesy of Hebe's Antiques

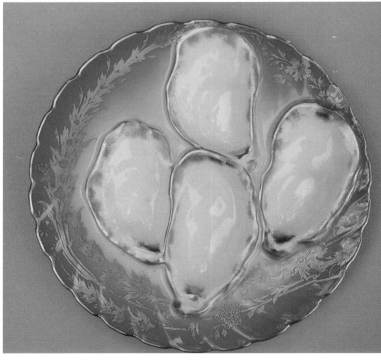

Haviland & Co.**
Limoges, France Made for Wright, Kay & Co., Detroit, MI
8 ⅜ inches
Courtesy of Hebe's Antiques

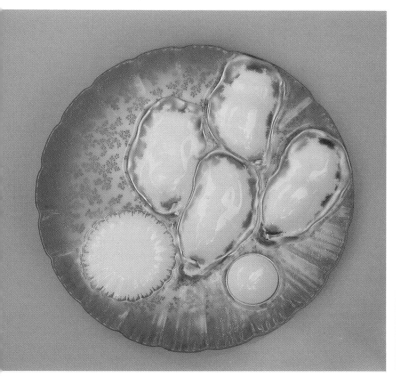

Haviland & Co.**
Limoges, France 9 inches
Courtesy of Hebe's Antiques

Unmarked**
8 ⅞ inches
Courtesy of Hebe's Antiques

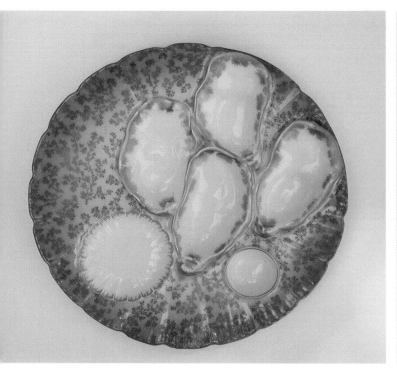

C. Ahrenfeldt**
Limoges, France Made for Higgins & Seiter, New York 9 ⅛ inches
Courtesy of Hebe's Antiques

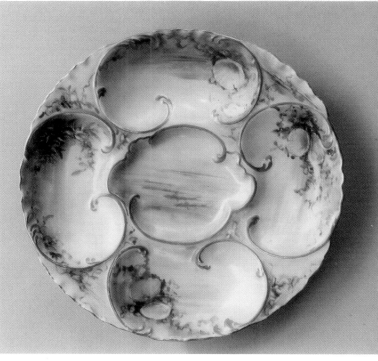

Unmarked***
7 ¾ inches
Courtesy of Hebe's Antiques

Unmarked***
8 inches
Courtesy of Hebe's Antiques

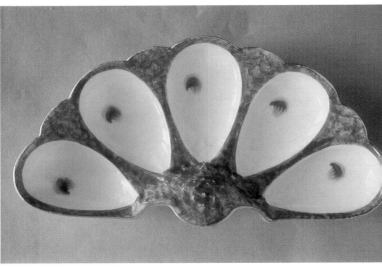

Charles Field Haviland***
Gerard, Dufraisseix and Morel Limoges, France 9 ¾ inches
Courtesy of Fisherman's Inn

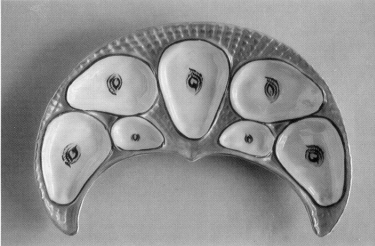

Unmarked***
10 ¼ inches
Courtesy of Fisherman's Inn

M. Redon***
Limoges, France 9 inches
Courtesy of Fisherman's Inn

Unmarked***
9 inches
Courtesy of Hebe's Antiques

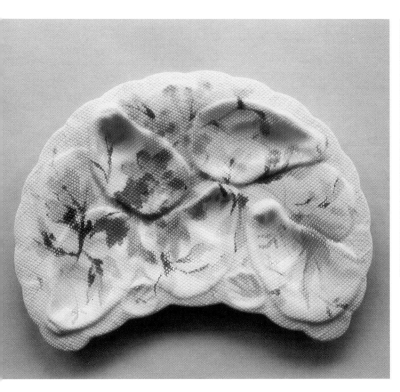

Unmarked***
9 inches
Courtesy of Hebe's Antiques

Unmarked***
9 inches
Courtesy of Hebe's Antiques

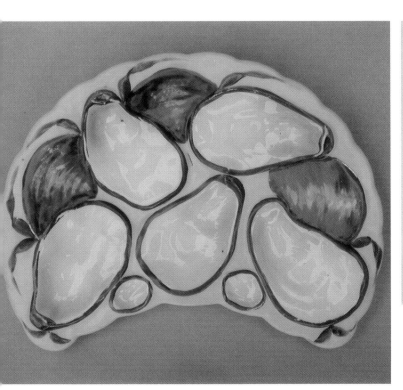

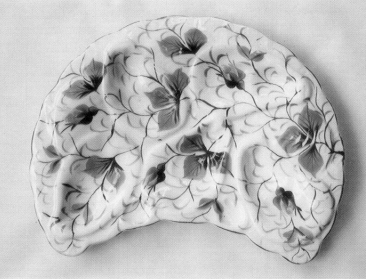

Unmarked***
9 inches
Courtesy of Hebe's Antiques

Unmarked***
9 inches
Roberta and Rudy Schmehl Collection

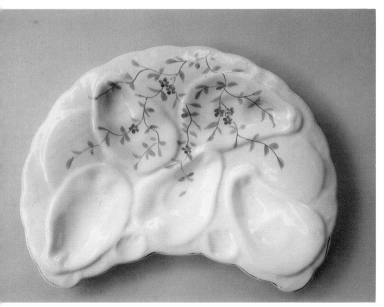

Unmarked***
9 inches
Courtesy of Hebe's Antiques

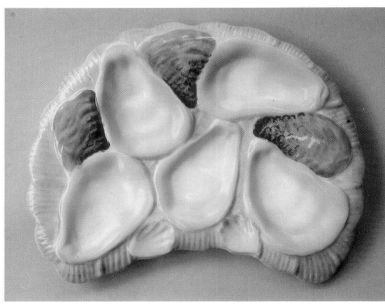

Unmarked***
9 inches
Courtesy of Hebe's Antiques

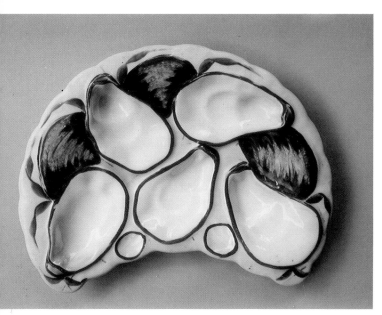

Unmarked***
9 inches
Courtesy of Hebe's Antiques

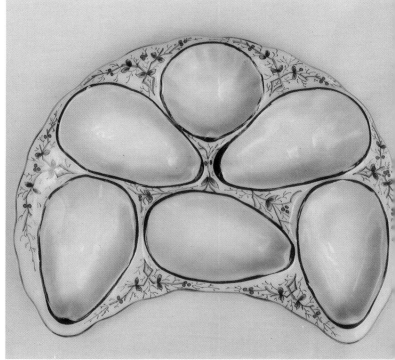

Unmarked***
9 inches
Courtesy of Hebe's Antiques

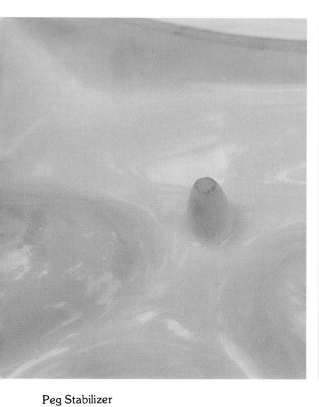

Peg Stabilizer

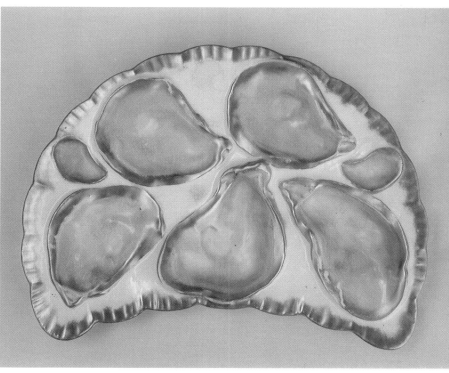

New England Pottery****
Boston, MA 9 inches
Courtesy of Hebe's Antiques

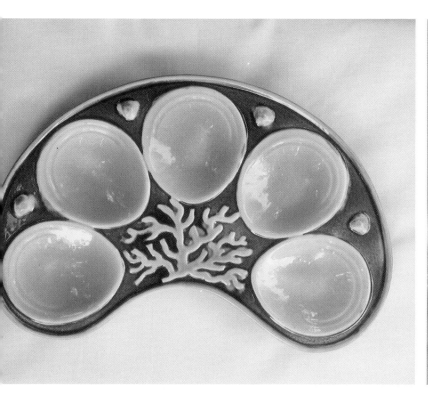

Unmarked***
10 inches
Courtesy of Hebe's Antiques

Logo for above

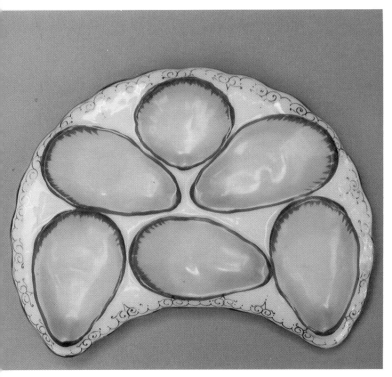

Unmarked***
9 inches
Courtesy of Hebe's Antiques

Charles Field Haviland**
Limoges, France 7 ½ inches

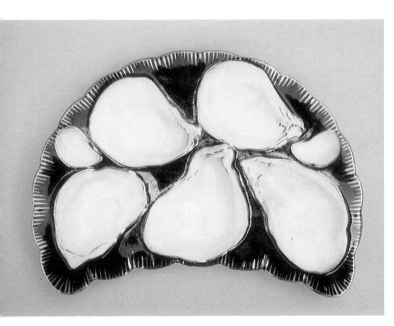

Mermod & Jaccard Jewelry Co.***
St. Louis, MO 9 ¼ inches
Courtesy of Hebe's Antiques

Charles Field Haviland**
Limoges, France 7 ½ inches
Courtesy of Hebe's Antiques

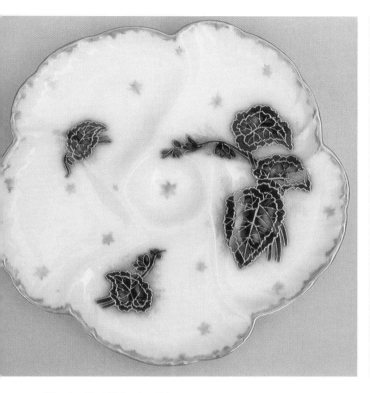

Charles Field Haviland**
Gerard, Duffraisseix and Morel Limoges, France 9 Inches
Courtesy of Hebe's Antiques

Tressemann & Vogt***
Limoges, France Made for Higgins & Seiter, New York, NY
8 inches
Courtesy of Fisherman's Inn

Unmarked**
8 ¼ Inches
Courtesy of Hebe's Antiques

Laviolette & Leonard***
Limoges, France 12 1/2 inches

Theodore Haviland**
Limogres France Made for S & G Gump, San Francisco, CA
8 ¼ inches
Courtesy of Hebe's Antiques

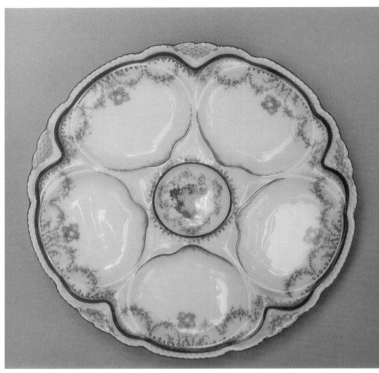

Theodore Haviland**
Limoges, France 8 ¼ inches
Courtesy of Hebe's Antiques

Logo for Above

Theodore Haviland**
Limoges, France 8 ⅜ inches
Courtesy of Fisherman's Inn

Theodore Haviland**
Limoges, France 9 ¼ inches
Courtesy of Wenger's Oyster House

Theodore Haviland**
Limoges, France Made for Higgins & Seiter, New York, NY
8 ¼ inches
Roberta and Rudy Schmehl Collection

Theodore Haviland**
Limoges, France 8 ¼ inches

Logo for Above

Theodore Haviland**
Limoges France 8 ¼ inches Made for Gienstass China Palace, Houston, TX
Courtesy of Hebe's Antiques

Theodore Haviland**
Limoges France Made for Burley & Co., Chicago, IL 8 ¼ inches

Logo for Above

Logo For Above

Haviland & Co.**
Limoges, France 9 inches
Courtesy of Hebe's Antiques

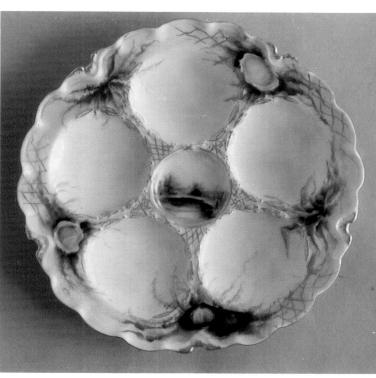

Haviland & Co.**
Limoges France 9 inches
Courtesy of Fisherman's Inn

Haviland & Co.**
Limoges, France 9 inches

Haviland & Co.**
Limoges, France Made for Wood, Bicknoll & Potter, Providence,
RI 9 inches
William M. Hodnik Collection

Haviland & Co.**
Limoges, France 9 inches
Courtesy of Fisherman's Inn

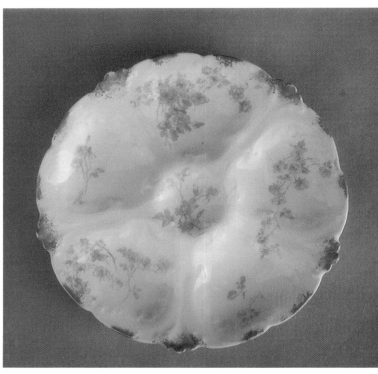

Gerard Dufraisseix & Abbot**
Limoges, France 7 ½ inches
Courtesy of Wenger's Oyster House

Oscar Gutherz***
Royal Austria C.T.Chase'08, Decorator 8 ⅝ inches
Courtesy of Fisherman's Inn

Mark & Gutherz***
Carlsbad 8 inches
Mary and Carlton Riggin Collection

Mark & Gutherz***
Carlsbad 9 inches
Courtesy of Hebe's Antiques

Unmarked***
10 inches
Courtesy of Hebe's Antiques

Unmarked***
7 ⅞ inches
Courtesy of Hebe's Antiques

Unmarked***
10 inches
Courtesy of Hebe's Antiques

Theodore Haviland & Co. Circa 1893★★★★
Limoges, France, Mont-Mery 8 ¾ inches
Courtesy of Evelyn Jones Antiques

Logo for Above, See Design Patent Number 22,117

Theodore Haviland & Co. Circa 1893****
Limoges, France, Mont-Mery 5 ½ inches
Courtesy of Hebe's Antiques

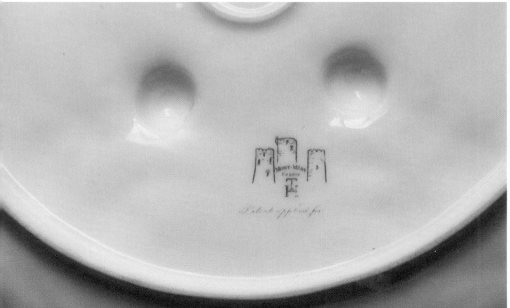

Logo for Above

Coiffe***
Limoges, France 8 ⅛ inches
Courtesy of Hebe's Antiques

Charles Field Haviland**
Gerard, Dufraisseix, and Morel Limoges France 9 inches
Courtesy of Hebe's Antiques

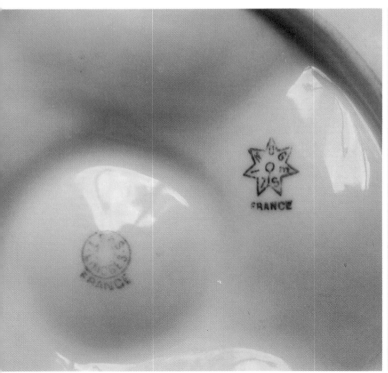

Logo for Above

Charles Field Haviland**
Gerard, Dufraissex, and Morel Limoges, France 9 inches
Courtesy of Wenger's Oyster House

Booth's Silicon China***
Tunstall, Staffordshire, England 8 ½ inches
Courtesy of Hebe's Antiques

Mark & Gutherz**
Carlsbad 8 ¾ inches
Roberta and Rudy Schmehl Collection

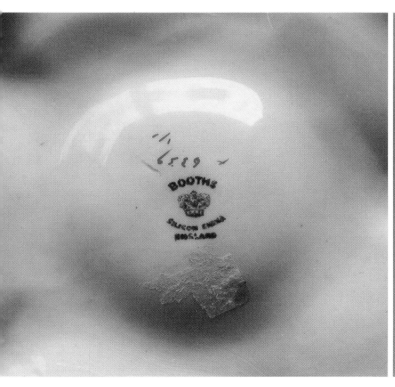

Logo for Above

Haviland & Co.**
Limoges, France Pour Tyndale, Mitchell Co., Philadelphia, PA
8 inches

M. Redon***
Limoges, France 8 ¼ inches
Courtesy of Hebe's Antiques

Unmarked***
8 ⅝ inches
Courtesy of Hebe's Antiques

Unmarked***
8 ⅝ inches
Courtesy of Hebe's Antiques

Tressemann & Vogt**
Limoges, France 8 ⅜ inches

Tressemann & Vogt***
Limoges, France Made for W.H. Plummer, New York 8 ½ inches
Courtesy of Hebe's Antiques

Haviland & Co.***
Limoges, France 8 ¾ inches
Courtesy of Hebe's Antiques

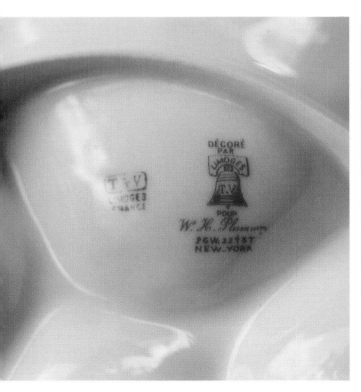

Logo for Above

Haviland & Co.**
Limoges, France For D.B. Bedell & Co. New York 8 ⅞ inches
Courtesy of Hebe's Antiques

Haviland & Co.***
Limoges, France 8 ¾ inches
Courtesy of Hebe's Antiques

Haviland & Co.**
Limoges, France For D.F. Richardson & Co. Detroit, MI 9 inches
Courtesy of Hebe's Antiques

Logo for Above

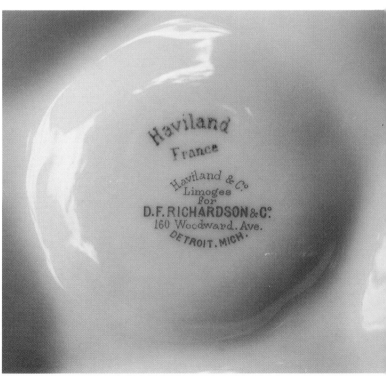

Logo for Above

Haviland & Co.★★★
Limoges, France Made for Steele Bros. Philadelphia, PA
8 ¾ inches
Courtesy of Hebe's Antiques

Haviland & Co.★★★
Limoges, France Made for Wright, Tyndale & Van Roden, Phila.,
PA 8 ¾ inches
Courtesy of Hebe's Antiques

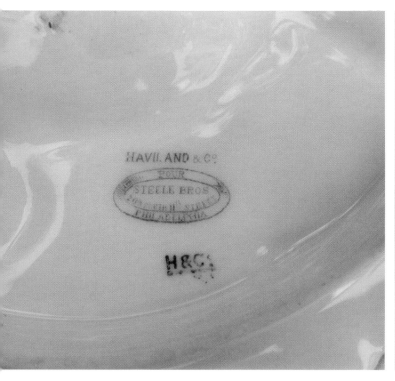

Logo for Above

Logo for Above

Haviland & Co.***
Limoges, France 8 ¾ inches
Roberta and Rudy Schmehl Collection

Wilhelm & Graef, NY***
10 inches
Courtesy of Hebe's Antiques

Haviland & Co.***
Limoges, France 8 ½ inches
Courtesy of Hebe's Antiques

Haviland & Co.***
Limoges France 7 ¾ inches
Courtesy of Hebe's Antiques

Gerard, Dufraisseix & Abbot**
Limoges, France 7 ½ inches
Courtesy of Hebe's Antiques

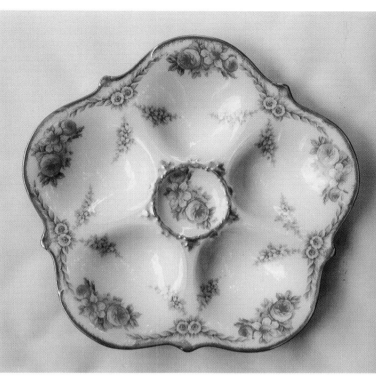

Bawo & Dotter**
Limoges, France 8 ¾ inches
Courtesy of Hebe's Antiques

Bawo & Dotter, Elite**
Limoges, France Made for Higgins & Seiter, New York 8 ¾ inches
Courtesy of Fisherman's Inn

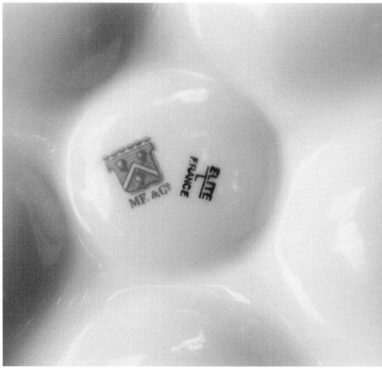

Logo for Above

Unmarked***
8 ¾ inches
Jean Wojciechowski Collection

Gerard, Dufraisseix & Abbot**
Limoges, France 7 ½ inches
Courtesy of Hebe's Antiques

C. Tielsch & Co.***
Silesia, Germany 9 ⅜ inches
Courtesy of Hebe's Antiques

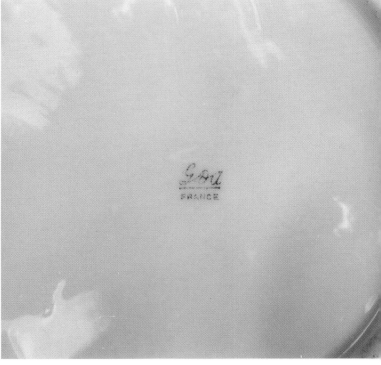

Logo for Above

Unmarked**
8 ½ inches
Courtesy of Hebe's Antiques

Unmarked***
8 ½ inches
Courtesy of Hebe's Antiques

Unmarked***
8 ½ inches
Courtesy of Hebe's Antiques

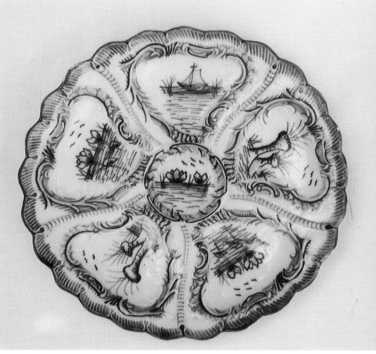

Unmarked**
8 ⅞ inches
Courtesy of Hebe's Antiques

Made for W.P. Helm & Chaef, New York**
9 ¼ inches
Courtesy of Fisherman's Inn

Theodore H. Haviland***
Limoges, France 8 ¼ inches
Courtesy of Hebe's Antiques

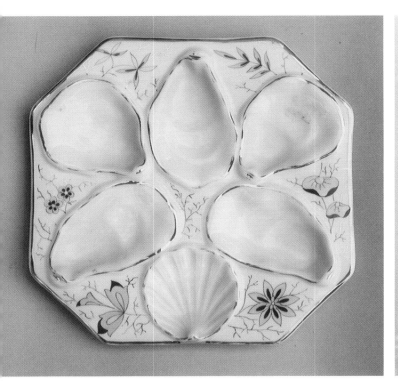

Unmarked**
8 ⅜ inches
Roberta and Rudy Schmehl Collection

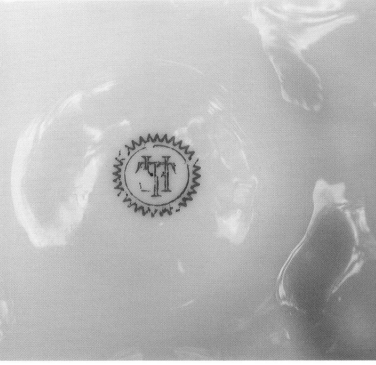

Logo for Above

Haviland & Co.***
Limoges, France Made for Wright, Kay & Co., Detroit, MI
8 ⅜ inches
Courtesy of Hebe's Antiques

Austrian***
8 inches
Courtesy of Fisherman's Inn

Haviland & Co.***
Limoges, France Made for Wright, Kay & Co., Detroit, MI
8 ⅜ inches
Courtesy of Hebe's Antiques

Unmarked**
7 ⅞ inches
Courtesy of Hebe's Antiques

Haviland & Co.***
Limoges France Made for Higgins & Seiter, New York 8 ⅛ inches
Courtesy of Hebe's Antiques

Made for Wright, Tyndale & Van Roden,***
Philadelphia, PA 8 inches
Courtesy of Hebe's Antiques

Unmarked***
9 ¼ inches
Courtesy of Hebe's Antiques

Unmarked**
10 ¾ inches
Courtesy of Hebe's Antiques

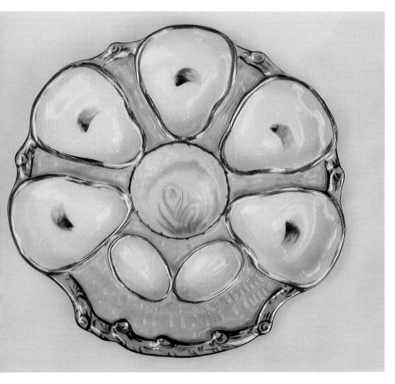

C. Tielsch★★★
9 ½ inches
Courtesy of Hebe's Antiques

Made in Germany★★
9 ½ inches
Courtesy of Hebe's Antiques

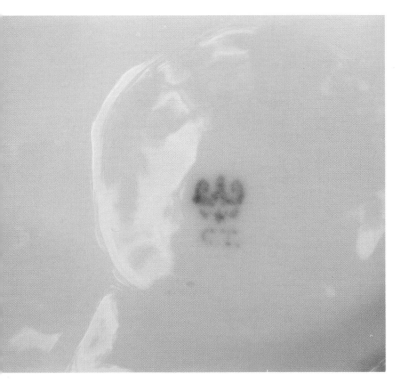

Logo for Avove

Unmarked★★
8 ⅜ inches
Courtesy of Hebe's Antiques

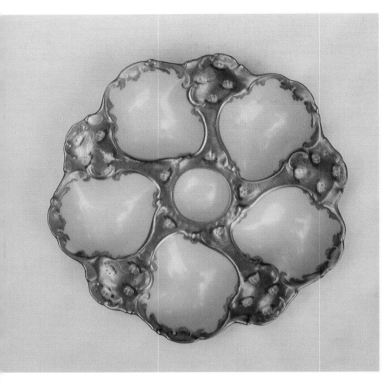

Tressemann & Vogt***
Patented December 22, 1896 Limoges, France Made for Davis,
Colamore & Co., New York 19 inches
Courtesy of Hebe's Antiques

Unmarked**
8 ¾ inches
Courtesy of Hebe's Antiques

Logo For Above

Unmarked***
9 inches
Courtesy of Fisherman's Inn

F. A. Mehlem Factory**
Germany 8 ⅝ inches
Courtesy of Hebe's Antiques

Unmarked**
8 ¾ inches
Courtesy of Hebe's Antiques

Unmarked, Cobalt Blue with
Folded Edge****
9 inches
Courtesy of Hebe's Antiques

Gerard, Dufraisseix & Abbot***
Limoges, France 8 ¾ inches
Jean Wojciechowski Collection

Charles Field Haviland***
Gerard, Dufraisseix & Morel Limoges, France 7 ½ inches
Courtesy of Hebe's Antiques

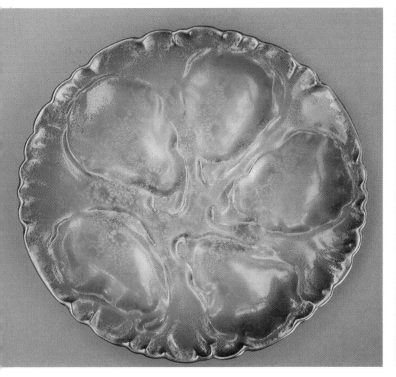

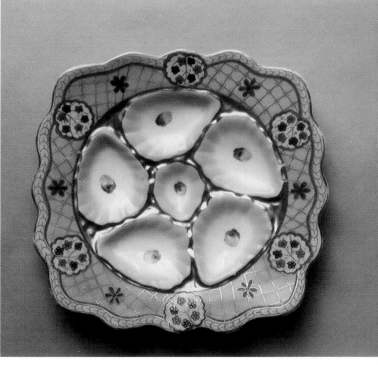

Haviland & Co.**
Limoges, France 7 ⅛ inches
Courtesy of Hebe's Antiques

Unmarked**
7 ½ inches
Courtesy of Hebe's Antiques

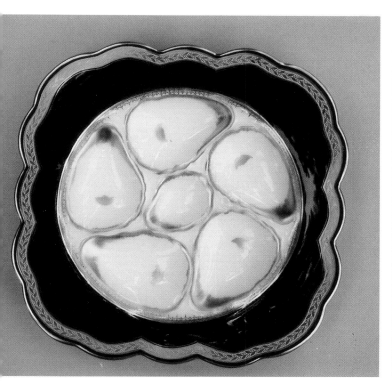

J.M.c D. S***
9 inches
Courtesy of Hebe's Antiques

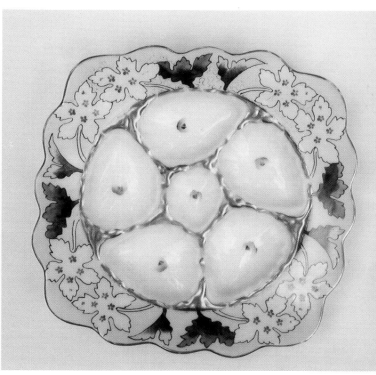

Mark & Gutherz***
Carlsbad 8 ⅞ inches
Courtesy of Hebe's Antiques

Logo for Above

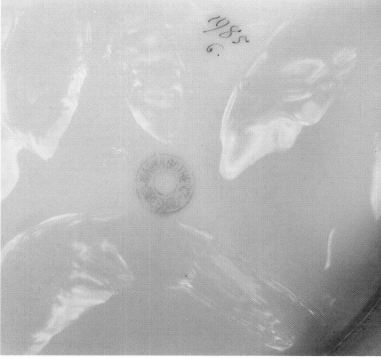

Logo for Above

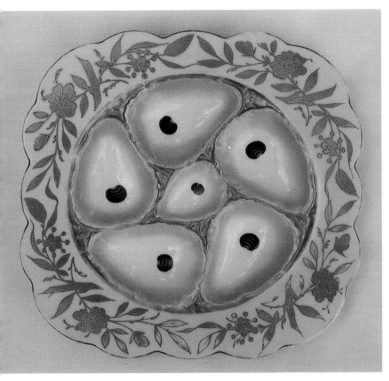

Unmarked**
8 ⅝ inches
Courtesy of Hebe's Antiques

Unmarked**
8 ⅝ inches
Courtesy of Hebe's Antiques

Unmarked**
8 ⅜ inches
Courtesy of Hebe's Antiques

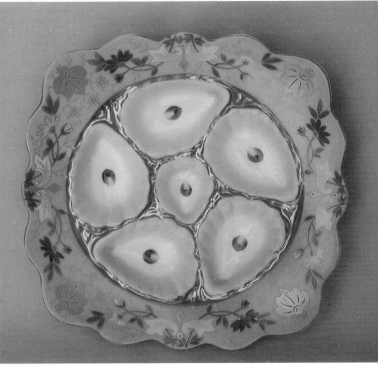

Mark & Gutherz***
Carlsbad 8 ⅝ inches
Roberta and Rudy Schmehl Collection

Unmarked**
8 ⅞ inches
Courtesy of Hebe's Antiques

Haviland & Co.***
Limoges, France Made for R. J. Allen Son & Co. Phila, PA 9 inches
Roberta and Rudy Schmehl Collection

Lewis Straus & Sons, New York Importers***
L S & S, Carlsbad 9 inches
Courtesy of Fisherman's Inn

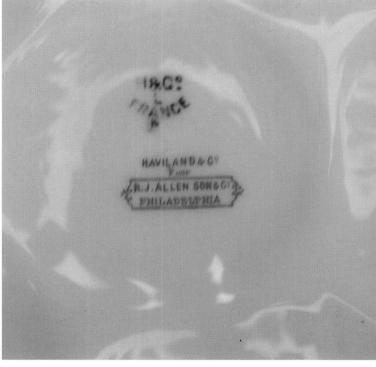

Logo For Above

Limoges, France**
9 inches
Jean Wojciechowski Collection

C.E. Carstens Porcelain Factory,***
Blankenhain, Germany, Weimar 8 ¼ inches
Courtesy of Wenger's Oyster House

Unmarked**
8 ⅜ inches
Courtesy of Fisherman's Inn

Unmarked**
8 ⅜ inches
Roberta and Rudy Schmehl Collection

Lewis Straus & Sons, New York Importers***
L S & S, Carlsbad 8 ½ inches
Courtesy of Fisherman's Inn

Oscar Gutherz***
Limoges, France 8 ½ inches
Roberta and Rudy Schmehl Collection

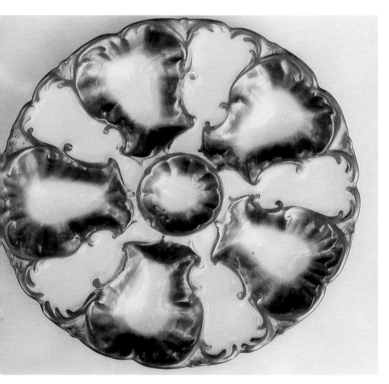

Lewis Straus & Sons, New York Importers**
L S & S, Carlsbad 8 ½ inches
Courtesy of Hebe's Antiques

Unmarked***
8 ⅜ inches
Courtesy of Hebe's Antiques

105

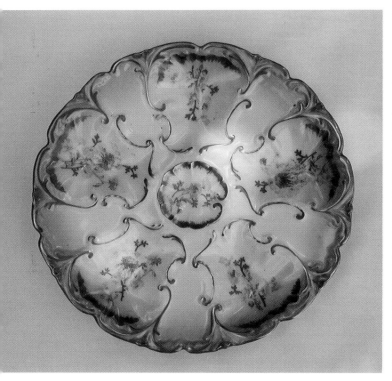

Lewis Straus & Sons, New York Importers***
L S & S, Carlsbad 8 ⅜ inches
Courtesy of Hebe's Antiques

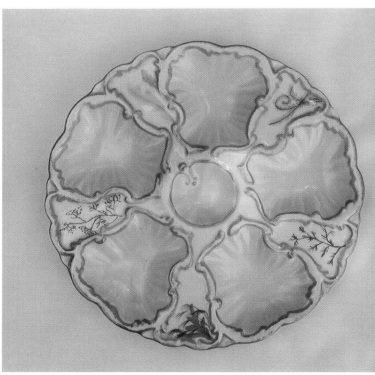

Unmarked**
8 ¾ inches
Courtesy of Hebe's Antiques

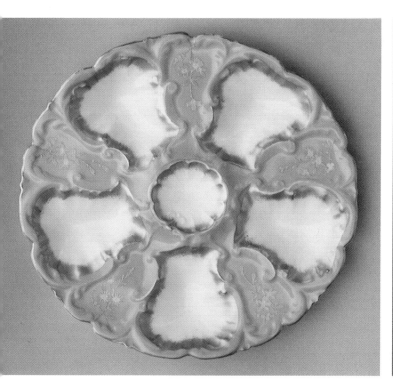

Lewis Straus & Sons, New York Importers***
L S & S, Carlsbad
Roberta and Rudy Schmehl Collection

C. & E. Carstens Porcelain Factory***
Blankenhain, Germany Weimar 9 ⅛ inches
Courtesy of Fisherman's Inn

Lewis Straus & Sons, New York Importers***
8 ½ inches
Courtesy of Hebe's Antiques

Limoges, France**
9 ½ inches
Courtesy of Hebe's Antiques

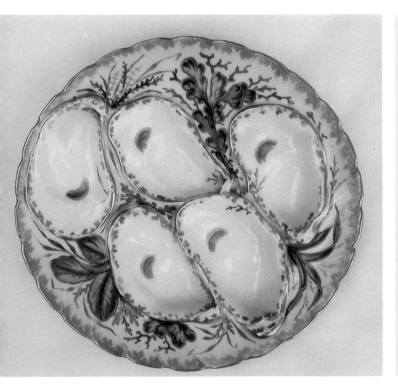

Haviland & Co.**
Limoges, France 7 ⅝ inches
Courtesy of Hebe's Antiques

Unmarked**
7 ¾ inches
Courtesy of Hebe's Antiques

Unmarked**
7 ¾ inches

Haviland & Co.**
Limoges France Made for J.E. Caldwell & Co., Phila PA 7 ¾ inches
Courtesy of Hebe's Antiques

R. Delinieres & Co.***
Limoges, France, D & Co. 7 ⅞ inches
Courtesy of Hebe's Antiques

Logo For Above

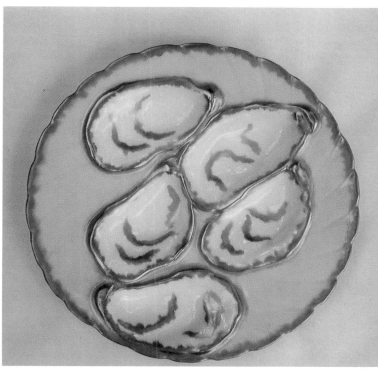

Haviland & Co.**
Limoges, France 7 ¾ inches Made for J.E. Caldwell & Co., Phila, PA

Haviland & Co.**
Limoges, France 7 ¾ inches
Courtesy of Hebe's Antiques

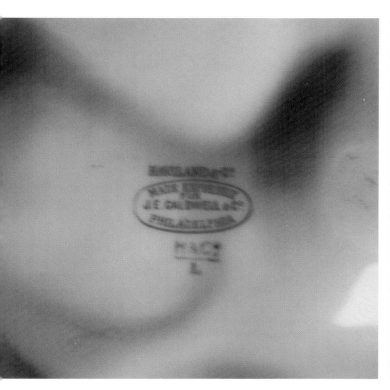

Logo for Above

Haviland & Co.***
Limoges, France 7 ¾ inches
Courtesy of Hebe's Antiques

Limoges, France***
Patented 1869 8 ½ inches
Courtesy of Hebe's Antiques

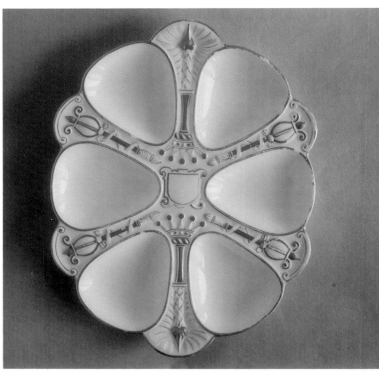

Unmarked***
8 ½ inches
Courtesy of Fisherman's Inn

Limoges, France***
8 ½ inches
Courtesy of Fisherman's Inn

Unmarked**
8 ¼ inches
Courtesy of Hebe's Antiques

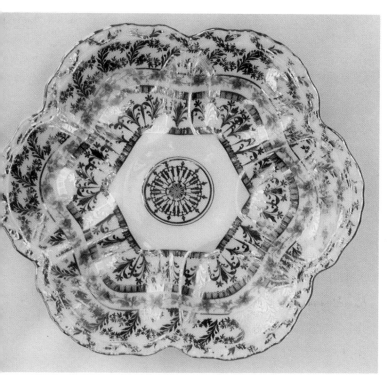

Austria***
Made for Higgins & Seiter, New York 8 ¾ inches
Courtesy of Hebe's Antiques

Haviland & Co.**
Limoges, France 8 ⅞ inches
Courtesy of Hebe's Antiques

Logo for Above

Unmarked**
9 inches
Courtesy of Hebe's Antiques

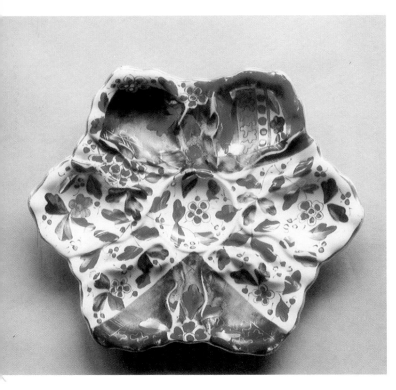

Unmarked**
9 ⅛ inches
Courtesy of Fisherman's Inn

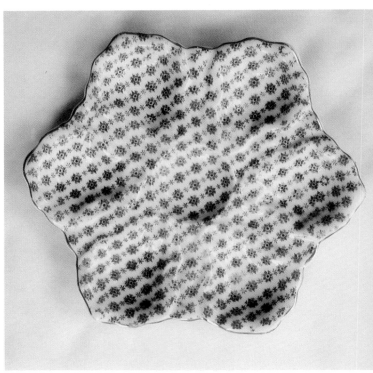

Blue Chintz**
9 ⅛ inches
Courtesy of Hebe's Antiques

Unmarked**
9 inches
Courtesy of Hebe's Antiques

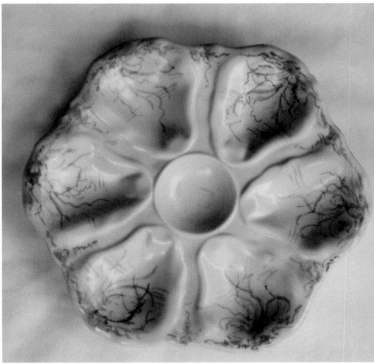

Unmarked**
9 ½ inches
Courtesy of Hebe's Antiques

Satsuma****
9 ⅛ inches
Courtesy of Hebe's Antiques
2/323 R53-35

Bottom of Above Showing Shell Feet

Satsuma****
9 ⅛ inches
Courtesy of Hebe's Antiques

Lazeyras, Rosenfeld and Lehman***
Limoges, France 9 ½ inches
Courtesy of Hebe's Antiques

England***
9 ½ inches by 9 inches
Courtesy of Hebe's Antiques

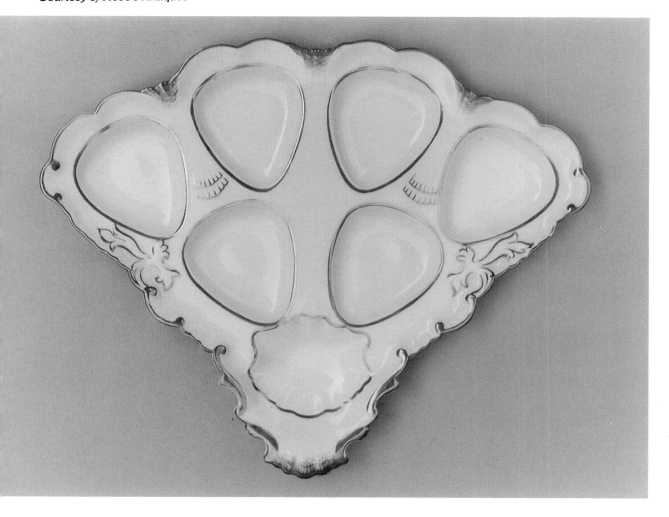

Charles Ahrenfeldt***
A La Pair Paris 9 ¾ inches
Courtesy of Hebe's Antiques

Royal Staffordshire Pottery***
Burslem, England 9 ¾ inches
Courtesy of Fisherman's Inn

Unmarked***
9 ½ inches
Courtesy of Fisherman's Inn

Logo for Above

Dresden***
Germany 9 inches
Courtesy of Fisherman's Inn

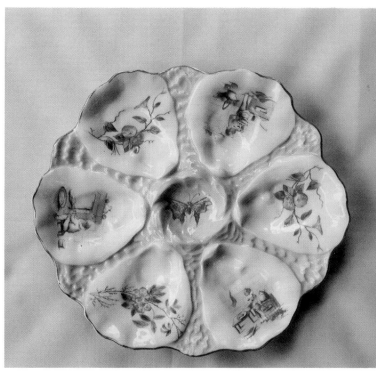

M. Redon***
Limoges, France 9 ½ inches
Courtesy of Hebe's Antiques

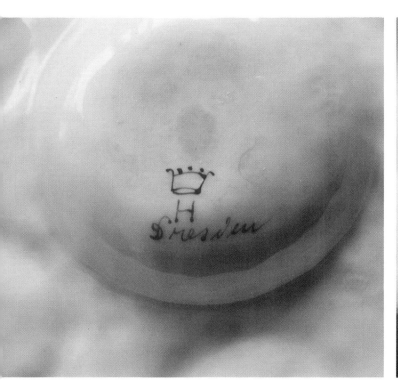

Logo for Above

Logo for Above

Victoria Porcelain Factory***
Bohemia, Czechoslovakia 8 ½ inches
Courtesy of Fisherman's Inn

Curtis Art Studio***
8 ½ inches
Courtesy of Hebe's Antiques

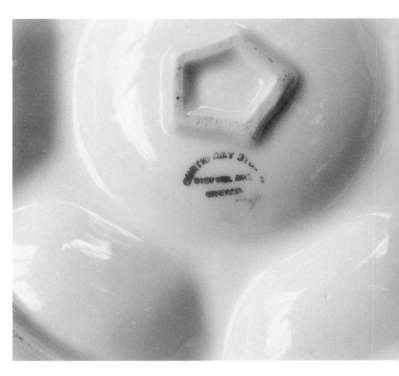

Logo For Above

Logo for Above

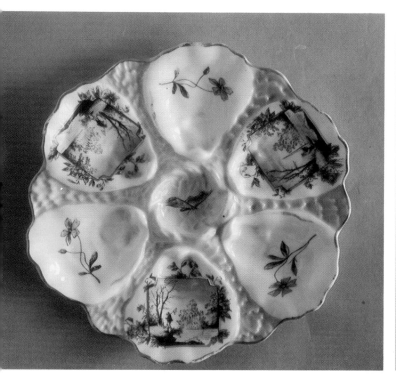

Theodore H. Haviland**
Limoges, France 9 ½ inches
Courtesy of Fisherman's Inn

Victoria Porcelain Factory***
Bohemia, Czechoslovakia 8 ⅝ inches
Courtesy of Fisherman's Inn

Unmarked**
8 inches
Courtesy of Hebe's Antiques

Unmarked***
9 ⅜ inches
Courtesy of Hebe's Antiques

B & H***
Limoges, France 9 ⅜ inches
Courtesy of Hebe's Antiques

Doulton***
Burslem, Staffordshire, England 8 ¾ inches
Courtesy of Hebe's Antiques

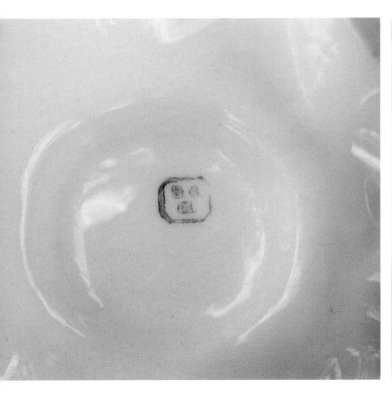

Logo for Above

Logo for Above

120

Haviland & Co.***
Limoges, France Made for Davis, Collamore & Co., New York
8 ¾ inches
Courtesy of Hebe's Antiques

Unmarked**
9 inches
Courtesy of Hebe's Antiques

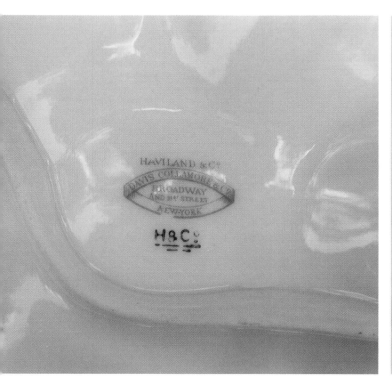

Logo for Above

Unmarked**
8 ⅞ inches
Courtesy of Hebe's Antiques

Unmarked**
8 ¾ inches
Courtesy of Hebe's Antiques

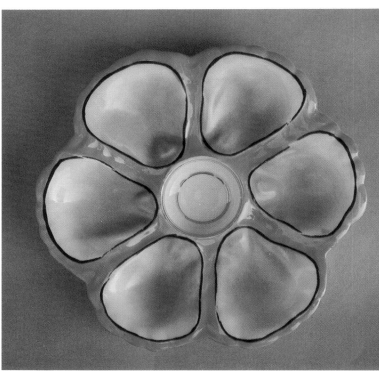

Unmarked**
9 inches
Courtesy of Wenger's Oyster House

Unmarked**
9 ¼ inches
Courtesy of Fisherman's Inn

C. Tielsch**
9 ¼ inches
Courtesy of Hebe's Antiques

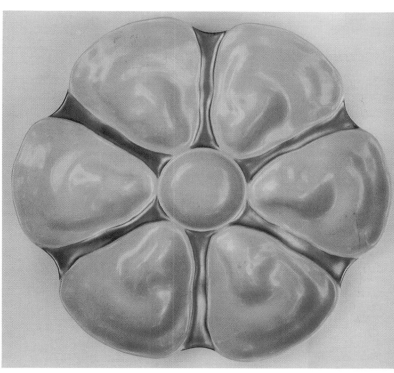

R. Delinieres & Co.***
D & Co, Limoges, France Made for Higgins & Seiter, New York
8 ¾ inches
Courtesy of Hebe's Antiques

Unmarked**
9 ½ inches
Courtesy of Hebe's Antiques

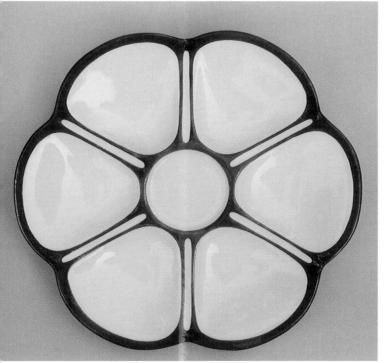

B & Co., Limoges, France**
L. Bernardaud & Co. Made for Higgins & Seiter 9 Inches
Courtesy of Hebe's Antiques

Unmarked**
9 ¼ inches
Courtesy of Hebe's Antiques

G. Mansard**
Paris, France 9 ½ inches
Courtesy of Hebe's Antiques

Unmarked**
9 ½ inches
Courtesy of Hebe's Antiques

G. Mansard**
Paris, France 9 ½ inches
Courtesy of Hebe's Antiques

Unmarked**
9 ¼ inches
Courtesy of Hebe's Antiques

Unmarked**
9 ⅝ inches
Courtesy of Evelyn Jones Antiques

Haviland & Co.***
Limoges, France 7 ¾ inches
Courtesy of Hebe's Antiques

Unmarked**
9 ⅝ inches
Courtesy of Evelyn Jones Antiques

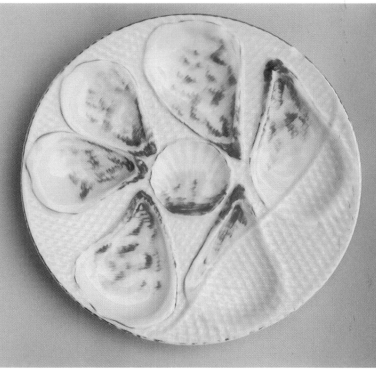

Unmarked***
8 ¼ inches
Roberta and Rudy Schmehl Collection

Minton, England***
8 ¾ inches
Courtesy of Hebe's Antiques

Haviland & Co.**
Limoges, France 9 ⅛ inches
Courtesy of Hebe's Antiques

E & B Napoli**
8 ½ inches
Courtesy of Hebe's Antiques

Haviland & Co.**
Limoges, France Made for H.B.Bedell & Co., New York
8 ⅝ inches
Courtesy of Hebe's Antiques

Minton, England****
8 ⅛ inches
Courtesy of Fisherman's Inn

Logo for Above

Lanternier***
Limoges, France 8 ¼ inches
Courtesy of Hebe's Antiques

Charles J. Ahrenfeldt***
Limoges, France Made for Serving on Ice on Half-Shell 9 ½ inches
Lisa Dorrell Collection

Logo for Above

Charles Ahrenfeldt***
Limoges, France Made for Serving on Ice on Half-Shell 7 ¾ inches

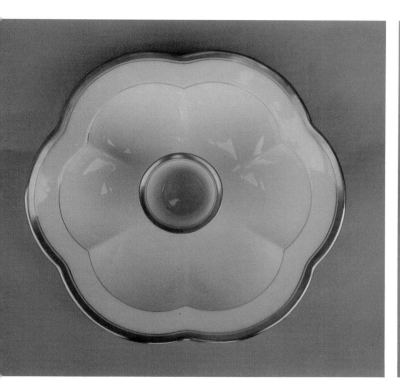

Lenox, Inc., Trenton, NJ**
8 ¾ inches, Separate Sauce Dish
Courtesy of Hebe's Antiques

Charles Ahrenfeldt***
Limoges, France Made for Higgins & Seiter, New York
9 ⅛ inches
Courtesy of Hebe's Antiques

Unmarked***
9 inches
Courtesy of Hebe's Antiques

Logo For Above

Haviland & Co.**
Limoges, France Amateur Decoration
8 ¾ inches
Lisa Dorrell Collection

Unmarked***
9 ⅜ inches
Roberta and Rudy Schmehl Collection

Tressemann & Vogt***
Limoges, France Made for Wilhelm & Graeff, New York
8 ⅞ inches
Jean Wojciechowski Collection

Unmarked**
8 ⅞ inches
Courtesy of Hebe's Antiques

Unmarked**
9 ½ inches
Roberta and Rudy Schmehl Collection

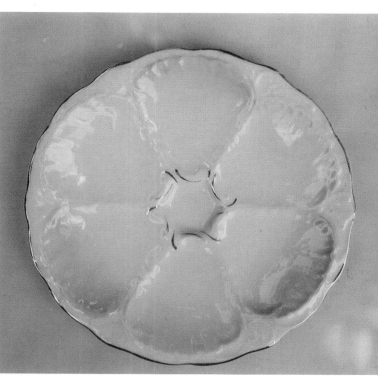

Unmarked**
8 inches
Courtesy of Hebe's Antiques

Unmarked**
8 ⅜ inches
Roberta and Rudy Schmehl Collection

Unmarked**
8 ¾ inches
Courtesy of Hebe's Antiques

Unmarked***
8 ¼ inches
Roberta and Rudy Schmehl Collection

Pressed Glass, Shell and Tassel Pattern***
10 inches
Courtesy of Stanley E. Dennis Antiques

Unmarked**
8 ⅛ inches
Courtesy of Hebe's Antiques

Made in France**
9 inches

Portugal**
9 ½ inches

Portieux, France**
8 ⅞ inches
Courtesy of Hebe's Antiques

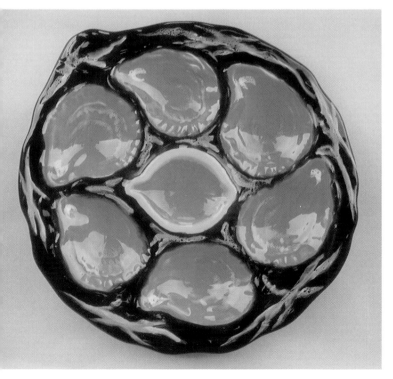

G.T.Faitman**
9 ¾ inches
Courtesy of Hebe's Antiques

Clear Pressed Glass**
9 ¼ inches
Courtesy of Hebe's Antiques

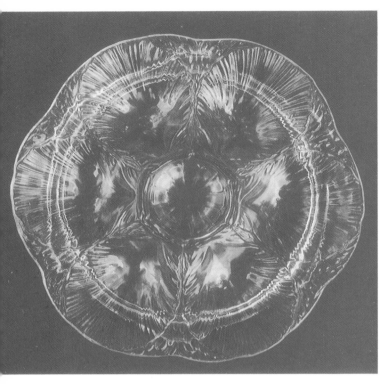

Clear Pressed Glass**
9 ½ inches
Courtesy of Hebe's Antiques

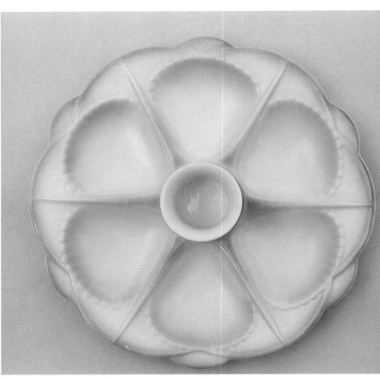

Made in Czechoslovakia**
Sauce Separate 9 inches

Gien, France**
9 ½ inches, with attached sauce dish
Courtesy of Hebe's Antiques

Made in Czechoslovakia**
9 inches
Courtesy of Hebe's Antiques

Hall Pottery**
Made in USA 10 ½ inches

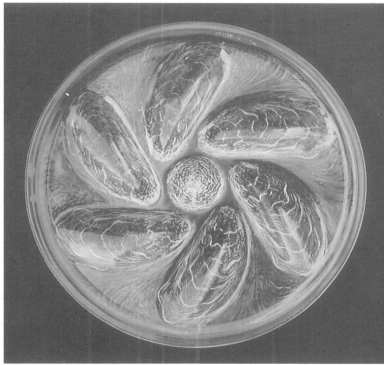

Arcoroc, France*
New Oyster Plate 10 ⅝ inches

Pewter*
Bonchef Augusta NJ 10 ½ inches

Other Specialized Plates

In addition to oyster plates, two other types of plates were designed to serve similar food. Snails, or *escargots,* as they are called in French, were served on a majolica plate designed for the purpose. The famous Terrapin stew, made from a type of turtle found in the same waters as oysters, also had specialized china. This dish was so desired that the supply of terrapin was almost exhausted causing the price to escalate beyond belief. Harvesting regulations were imposed making the stew unavailable until recently, but most people have forgotten about it. Plates with these designs are sometimes found with oyster plate collections.

When acquiring plates for a personal collection, the author's encourage choosing what pleases you. If you want to include plates of later manufacture because of their attractiveness, do so. If you wish to have only antique plates, remember that there is no substitute for knowledge. If you haven't the time or inclination to study the field yourself, pick reliable dealers as the best alternative. Communicate your needs and follow their advice. To determine the manufacturer or approximate date of manufacture, the student should refer to the reference books on specific pottery marks and manufacturers, some listed in the bibliography.

Portugal, Majolica***
Escargot Plate 10 ¾ inches
Courtesy of Hebe's Antiques

Escargot Plate***
10 inches
Courtesy of Hebe's Antiques

Diamond Back Terrapin Stew Bowl****
Edwin J.D. Boodley Burslem, England 7 ⅞ inches
Courtesy of Fisherman's Inn

Back of Terrapin Stew Bowl

Portugal*
Oyster Shaped Majolica Soup Toureen

Silver Serving Pieces

In addition to plates used to serve oysters, a whole variety of sterling and silver-plated serving pieces came into being. Oyster forks appeared in hotels and restaurants before 1860, and as silver companies expanded their lines, ladles for serving oyster stew, forks for fried oysters, oyster servers, and a combination oyster fork-spoon appeared. Hotels and restaurants first used these pieces, but they soon appeared in homes, being sold by local china and jewelery stores because demand was created when they were seen in the public places. By 1900, a proper single place setting required eight pieces, and a complete service for eighteen including serving pieces consisted of over four hundred items. Even a special French Muscadet wine was made to be served with oysters!

The following poem was published October 12, 1889 in the *Detroit Free Press*:

Let us royster with the oyster—in the shorter days and moister, That are brought by brown September, with its rogish final R; For breakfast or for supper, on the shell or upper, Of dishs he's the daisy, and of shell-fish he's the star. We try him as they fry him, and even as they pie him; We're partial to him luscious in a roast; And O he is delicious stewed with toast. We eat him with tomatoes, and the salad with potatoes, Nor look him o'er with horror when he follows the cold slaw; And neither does he fret us if he marches after lettuce And abreast of cayenne pepper when his majesty is raw. So welcome with September to the knife and glowing ember. Juicy darling of our dainties, dispossessor of the clam! To the oyster, then, a hoister, with him a royal royster We shall whoop it through the land of heathen jam!

Muscadet Wine Served with Oysters

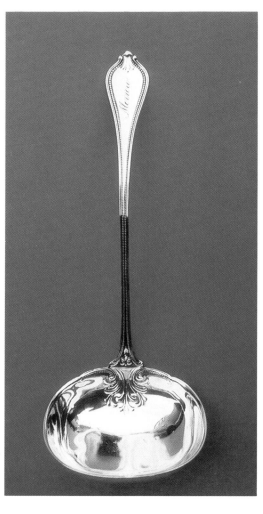

Towle Silversmith's, Old Newbury Pattern**
Silver Oyster Ladle, 10 inches

Spoon From Union Oyster House**
Boston, MA
Bill and Steve Dorrell Collection

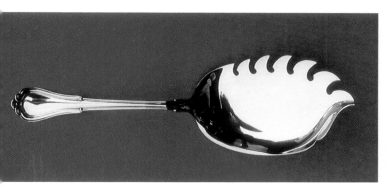

Gorham Silversmiths, Norfolk Pattern***
Silver Fried Oyster Fork, 8 ½ Inches

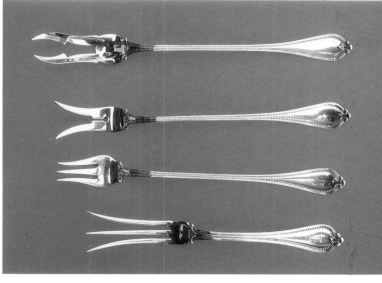

Wood & Hughes, New York****
Silver Oyster Serving Spoon, 10 inches, Note Tunnel in handle for
Juices to Run Back into Bowl

Lobster Fork, Lemon Fork,**
Oyster Cocktail Fork, Lemon Fork

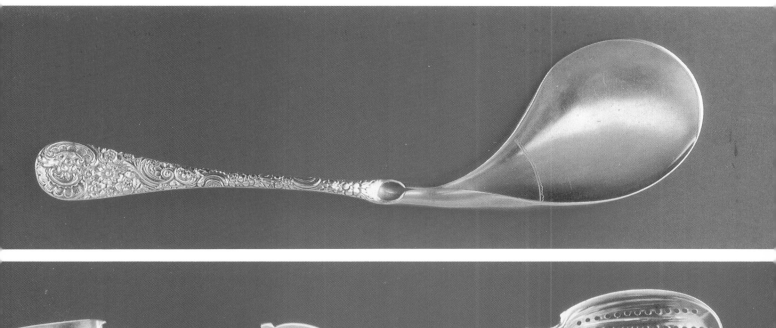

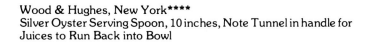

Coin silver oyster fork/spoon. 9 ½", monogrammed "D."*****

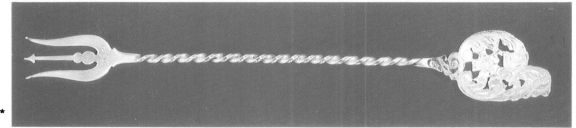

Silver Oyster Fork/Spoon***
8 ¼ Inches

Restaurants

Restaurants specializing in oysters are few today, although some old-line establishments with nostalgia and ambiance survive in larger cities. Some of the old ones display collections of oyster memorabilia, especially plates, but their menus usually carry only a few oyster dishes, and they probably are not served on the traditional plates. The Sansom Street Oyster House in Philadelphia, the Oyster Bar in New York City's Grand Central Terminal, and the Union Oyster House in Boston are a few traditional restaurants that come to mind. The Sansom Street Oyster House has a large collection of oyster plates on display and serves oysters of many varieties, including the French Belon. Smaller towns also have their establishments. At Kent Narrows in Grasonville, Maryland the Fisherman's Inn has a great display of oyster plates and The Harris Crab House displays a large number of oyster cans.

Fisherman's Inn Kent Narrows, Grasonville, MD

Harris Crab House Kent Narrows, Grasonville, MD

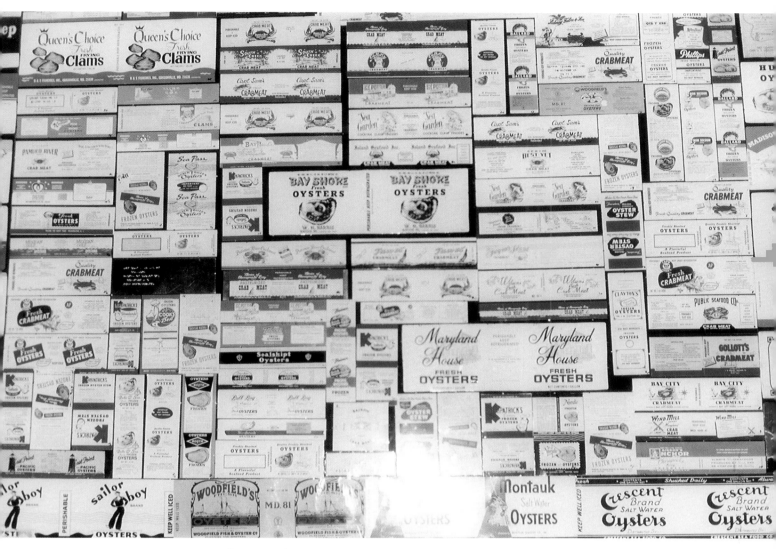

Display of Oyster Can Bodies at Harris Crab House

One of the few surviving typical smalltown oyster houses is Wenger's Oyster House in Reading, Pennsylvania. The first generation of this family in the oyster business served oysters in Terre Hill, Pennsylvania, but Joseph Wenger moved the business to downtown Reading in 1927. The next generation, Ross Wenger, moved the oyster house to the edge of town, and today it is located in the suburbs to stay close to their customers. In a newspaper article about Wenger's Oyster House, it is reported that in the 1920s and 1930s twelve hundred oysters were served here each day, and Joseph Wenger is said to have opened 10,000,000 oysters during his time in the business. Today, Wayne Deswart manages the restaurant, continuing the tradition.

Oyster plates are no longer popular in restaurants because of the problem in stacking them. They are very unstable and chip easily when piled upon each other. Most plates have a circular foot on the bottom for stability. When stacked, this foot touched the divisions of the plate underneath causing chips. Some manufacturers have broken the ring into segments or placed pointed extensions at intervals to facilitate stacking.

The usual gold trim on oyster plates is easily washed away when dishwashers are used, adding to the problem. Felt or foam padding can be placed between the plates when stored, and only mild soap should be used when washing them. If plate hangers are used to display the dishes, the prongs of these hangers may chip the edges of the plates. Undamaged plates with all their gold decoration are valuable, while less than perfect plates generally are not a good investment.

Wenger's Oyster and Seafood House, Shillington, PA

Newspaper Article of Joe Wenger

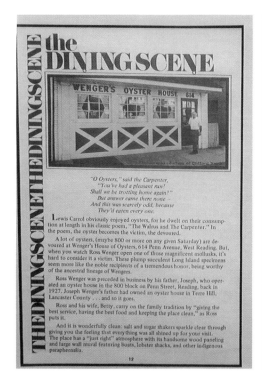

the DINING SCENE

THEDININGSCENETHEDININGSCENE

"O Oysters," said the Carpenter,
"You've had a pleasant run!
Shall we be trotting home again?"
But answer came there none —
And this was scarcely odd, because
They'd eaten every one.

Lewis Carrol obviously enjoyed oysters, for he dwelt on their consumption at length in his classic poem, "The Walrus and The Carpenter." In the poem, the oyster becomes the victim, the devoured.

A lot of oysters, (maybe 800 or more on any given Saturday) are devoured at Wenger's House of Oysters, 614 Penn Avenue, West Reading. But, when you watch Ross Wenger open one of those magnificent mollusks, it's hard to consider it a victim. These plump succulent Long Island specimens seem more like the noble recipients of a tremendous honor, being worthy of the ancestral lineage of Wengers.

Ross Wenger was preceded in business by his father, Joseph, who operated an oyster house in the 800 block on Penn Street, Reading, back in 1927. Joseph Wenger's father had owned an oyster house in Terre Hill, Lancaster County . . . and so it goes.

Ross and his wife, Betty, carry on the family tradition by "giving the best service, having the best food and keeping the place clean," as Ross puts it.

And it is wonderfully clean: salt and sugar shakers sparkle clear through giving you the feeling that everything was all shined up for your visit. The place has a "just right" atmosphere with its handsome wood paneling and large wall mural featuring boats, lobster shacks, and other indigenous paraphernalia.

Of special interest, is a collection of antique (turn of the century) "on the half shell" dishes which are housed in two lighted display nooks. Polished wooden tables and chairs enhance the setting, and a bar with stools completes it.

One look at the menu, "Bill of Fare", and you are pleasantly surprised at the versatility of the oyster and his sister (brother?) mollusk, the clam. Fried oysters come by the numbers: three, four, or a half-dozen. You are offered a choice of bread crumb or cracker crumb padding — the bread crumb is heavier and darker after cooking, while the cracker is light and dryer. And conventional lunchers won't feel slighted; there are oyster and fish sandwiches available.

When you order fried oysters at Wengers, you don't have to probe around inside a fried crumb container looking for the oyster. The padding merely compliments the star of the show, the oyster.

Fried clams are also ordered by the number and again the choice of padding. For variety, the menu offers crab cakes, deviled clams, scallops, flounder stuffed with crab meat, shrimp stuffed with crab meat, and shrimp butterfly.

Oysters and clam (on the half shell) cocktails are available in blue point and large oysters and little necks and medium clams. Hot sauce comes by the water pitcher at Wenger's for easy pouring of individual orders. Hot clam broth is preferred as an accompaniment by many and comes by the cup.

Would you believe three different oyster stews? The regular is made with the smaller oyster, the Boston features the addition of toast, and the Box stew boasts the large mollusk. Clam stew comes in the same varieties.

Wenger's stews are a meal in themselves, a most compatable mixture of just the right amount of broth and just enough vegetables served in a mini-turren sired bowl.

There are also pan oyster and clam stews which Ross explained are made with broth instead of the milk base. Clam chowder (Manhattan style) is also available. Take out orders of any menu item by request.

To round out your meal, there are French fries, applesauce, pie, and pepper

Story of Wenger's Oyster House

CHAPTER THREE
Oyster Plate Manufacturers

AMERICA

Union Porcelain Works

In America, the first company to make oyster plates was the Union Porcelain Works of Greenpoint, New York. Established by German potters about 1854, this company was purchased later by C.H.L. Smith and Thomas C. Smith. Thomas Smith and Sons registered a logo consisting of an eagle's head with the letter "S" in its beak in 1877. This logo, along with the letters U.P.W. and a patent date of September 10,'78 appears on most of their oyster plates. There are two sizes of clam shaped plates and one round plate. Around 1900, the company moved to Brooklyn, New York, where it manufactured porcelain insulators. Union Porcelain Works oyster plates are being reproduced today with a much larger mark than the originals stamped with black ink. This reproduction mark is easily recognized.

Phoenixville Pottery, Kaolin and Firebrick Company

Majolica ware became popular in America because it was inexpensive and available in many different pieces. Some of the best of American majolica was made by the Phoenixville Pottery, Kaolin and Firebrick Company of Phoenixville, Pennsylvania. Begun in 1867, this company went through several changes in ownership and by 1879 was known as Griffin, Smith and Hill. On January 1, 1879, a partnership was formed among brothers Henry R. and George S. Griffin, David Smith and William Hill. Their logo was designed with the four names, but before majolica was made William Hill withdrew from the company. The remaining partners used the original logo on their Etruscan Majolica oyster plates. These have a beautiful design and today are very rare, only a few examples are known among collectors. The designer for this pottery was Mr. Bourne, an artist who used themes from nature in his work. The company also made the well-known shell and seaweed pattern and won several gold medals at the Cotton Centennial Exposition in New Orleans in 1884. Although Griffin, Smith and Hill closed in 1892, the buildings were used later by other pottery makers.

EUROPE

Like all imports to the United States after 1891, oyster plates made abroad were marked with their countries of origin. That year, the United States enacted the McKinley Tariff Law stating that all articles imported must include the country where they were made. Therefore, plates made after 1891 and imported to the United States for sale will bear the name of the country where they were made.

FRANCE

Limoges

In Europe, oyster plates were made by companies throughout England, France, Germany and Eastern Europe.

Many potters settled in Limoges, France because the area contained ideal natural resources for fine porcelain. A wide range of dinner sets was made in the town and is marked LIMOGES. Limoges china had a lovely color and gold trim. If the word *Depose* appears on this china, it means "patented" in French. They are still making the china, but the details and gold trim are not as elaborate as on the older pieces.

Haviland and Company

The city of Limoges, France is well-known for china and one of the most prominent manufacturers is Haviland & Company. In 1842, David Haviland, a New York china importer, moved to Limoges because local clay was suitable for fine china. At this time the mark used was "H & Co." and "Haviland & Co." After this period, there were two marks on the china, one for the factory and one for where the piece was decorated. As United States importers placed special orders for clients such as department stores and railroads, the clients' name was placed on the back as well. White manufacturer's marks are found under the glaze while decoration marks are found over the glaze.

David Haviland's three sons, Charles, Edward and Theodore, took various interests in the pottery. Theodore left the firm to start his own business. In 1852, a nephew, Charles Field Haviland, was sent to Limoges by his father to learn the pottery business from his uncle. When Charles Field Haviland took over, he used his name or initials CFH. This mark is common on oyster plates. After the company name was changed to Gerard, Dufraisseix and Morel in 1881, the initials were used for the following ten years. When David died in 1879, the firm was passed to his sons, Charles and Edward. Theodore Haviland of New York later bought out his brothers and combined the companies. Therefore, different maker's marks exist, including "Haviland, France;" "Haviland & Co.," "Limoges" and "Decorated by Haviland & Co."

Quimper

Quimper pottery is named for the town of Quimper, France. The first potter settled there in 1685 and later other rival pottery factories were begun. In the 19th century, potters started using scenes with Breton characters on their oyster plates. In 1884, Jules Henroit took over the Dumaine factory and added to his company. Another factory in Quimper was Hubaudiere-Bousquet, which used the mark "HB". The Quimper pieces made during the late 1880s are exceptional, including a three-tiered oyster server. Quimper plates have the "HR", "HR Quimper" and the "HB" marks. Pieces made about 1920 and later are not considered as desirable as the earlier pieces. Quimper pottery is still made today and some of the older pieces are being reproduced. Modern pieces are marked, like other reproductions, with paper labels that are easily removed.

Sarreguemines

Utzchneider & Co. was a factory established in Sarreguemines, France in the late 18th century by Paul Utzchneider and M. Fabray. They copied many of the Wedgwood decorations and the mark was, in capital letters, "SARREGUEMINES." This company is still in operation.

ENGLAND

If one collects china made in England, it is necessary to notice the registry marks found on the backs of the plates. This is a diamond shaped mark, found on all decorative art designs, used from 1843 to 1883. It indicates the material, day, month and year of manufacture. Tables of registry symbols can be found in reference books to interpret the mark.

Minton

Thomas Minton built a small pottery at Stoke-on-Trent, Staffordshire, England in 1793 which made porcelain and tiles. When Thomas died in 1836, his son Herbert took charge. By employing new techniques, he became one of the largest porcelain producers of his time. In 1849, Leon Arnoux was hired as the art director and developed wonderful colored majolica pieces. The Minton pieces were designed by many famous artists using leaves, shells, seaweed, fish, flowers and animals. In additon to oyster plates, Minton made sardine boxes, asparagus dishes and many animal covered pieces. Prior to 1873, the company used a globe with a crown mark and the word "MINTONS" across the middle of the globe. After 1873, the "s" was dropped and the globe was used with the word "MINTON" across the middle.

A new oyster plate has been recorded with the globe mark, "Mintons" in the center, and all printed in black. There is no substitute for knowledge.

Holdcroft

Little is known about Joseph Holdcroft majolica except that it was made about 1870-1885 at Daisy Bank in Longton, England. The detail on his majolica is excellent and many oyster plates have been found. The company marked majolica "JHOLDCROFT" in block letters and a "J H" monogram.

George Jones & Sons Ltd.

George Jones worked for Minton for many years before establishing his company in 1861 at Stoke-on-Trent. In 1873 the company name was changed to George Jones & Sons, Ltd. They used the monogram "J" through a "G" enclosed in a circle. The registry mark is found on many George Jones pieces. The majolica made by this company was perfect in every detail. His duplication of natural phenomenon indicates a tremendous amount of research to produce the design.

Wedgwood

Josiah Wedgwood of England was one of the best known potters of his time and his pieces were functional as well as ornamental. In 1744, after the death of his father, also a potter, he worked for his brother Thomas. After an apprenticeship of five years, he wanted to continue experimentation but his brother disagreed. He went into partnership with Thomas

Whieldon in 1754 which worked out very well. Finally, he went into business for himself in 1759 and was ahead of his time in manufacturing and marketing techniques. He eventually became the most influential person ever in the history of English pottery. His love of nature and intellectual curosity lead Josiah Wedgwood to produce majolica in 1860. Wedgwood made many unusual pieces including a pattern of shell and seaweed, and his oyster plates are clearly the most ambitious with fish between the openings of the wells and a great amount of detail. Most of the dishes are marked "WEDGWOOD." The family tradition of manufacturing Majolica china continued until 1910.

S. Fielding & Co., Ltd.

S. Fielding & Co. Ltd., located at Stoke-on-Trent, England, made majolica plates from 1878 to 1900. An unusual oyster plate is star centered, surrounded by six oyster shaped indentations, and marked "FIELDING" in block letters. His textured backgrounds and oriental influence made his plates unusual.

Doulton

In 1877, Henry Doulton bought a pottery located in Burslem, Staffordshire, England. A large group of artists was hired by Doulton to improve the quality of their production. Charles Noke came to work for the company in 1889 and proved to be a great asset. Most of the oyster plates manufactured by the Doulton company are marked DOULTON over BURSLEM.

Worcester Royal Porcelain Company Ltd

The Worcester pottery, established in 1751, changed greatly until the Victorian era. In 1862 the Worcester Royal Porcelain Company, Ltd. was formed by Messrs Kerr and Binns. By the 1870s, artist James Hadley made some of their first porcelains. Until the 1920s, the company produced some of the finest china of the time. Today, other companies reproduce Worcester porcelain, especially oyster plates.

GERMANY

There were more than 250 porcelain factories located in Germany during the nineteenth and twentieth centuries. Many oyster plates are marked with WEIMAR (Germany) and a crown over a shield with "Weimar" diagonally crossing the shield.

Meissen

The Meissen porcelain factory was founded in Meissen, Germany about 1710 and their distinctive crossed swords mark was adopted in 1723. This mark was later copied by many other factories.

Dresden

Between about 1895 and 1910, when oyster plates were very popular, factories in the German city of Dresden started making porcelain in the Meissen style. Various pieces of Meissen porcelain were taken home by employees of the company and painted, making it difficult to authenticate them today. Helena Wolfson, for example, a decorator in Dresden, copied the mark of "A R Meissen" pieces and trained her staff to imitate the painting style of the Meissen china. She also purchased blanks from the Meissen factory for her staff to decorate. She was made to cease making the pieces with the mark "HR." In 1880, the word "Dresden" with a D and a crown mark was used on Dresden plates.

AUSTRIA

Some oyster plates are marked "Victoria, Austria." Many Austrian pieces are classified with Bohemian (eastern European) porcelain which developed in the late 19th century and include tableware and decorative pieces.

Carlsbad

Since Carlsbad was the center of the porcelain factories in Austria, many of the potteries used the name Carlsbad in their marks. These pieces are easily recognized and include a great many oyster plates.

CZECHOSLOVAKIA

Moser

Ludwig Moser founded a glass polishing and engraving workshop in Karlsbad, Czechoslovakia, in 1857. Moser glass included lovely designs with an additional layer of glass on top. Moser glass oyster plates are quite beautiful. One plate illustrated in this book is colored green, another purple, and still onother clear with raised lemons in the middle of the oyster wells. The design is different and appealing.

U.S. Design Patents

The design patent papers in the U.S. Patent Office in Washington, D.C. contain design patents for various oyster plates that were taken out by many individuals. J.W. Boteler of Washington, D.C., received the first patent in the United States for an oyster plate design, number 7491, on June 16, 1874. His plate had the expected indentations, but was made different by its handle. When actually produced, the handle style was changed, but the design is basically the same as patented.

Each designer attempted to produce, advertise and sell plates different from their competition. Interestingly, several of the patent papers state that their design was new, original and ornamental.

UNITED STATES PATENT OFFICE.

JOHN W. BOTELER, OF WASHINGTON, DISTRICT OF COLUMBIA.

DESIGN FOR OYSTER-DISHES.

Specification forming part of Design No. 7,491, dated June 16, 1874; application filed June 2, 1874.
[Term of Patent 3½ years.]

To all whom it may concern:

Be it known that I, JOHN W. BOTELER, of the city of Washington, in the District of Columbia, have invented a Design for Oyster-Dishes, of which the following is a specification:

The nature of my design is fully represented in the accompanying drawing, to which reference is made; and it consists of a dish or plate for serving up oysters, &c., and is made in imitation of half oyster-shells.

In the drawing, A A A A represent four receptacles for receiving the oysters. They are made in imitation of half oyster-shells. B is a lemon, salt, or pepper receiver, and C is a handle for carrying the plate or dish.

I prefer to make the dish or plate of the form represented; but I do not consider this exact shape an essential element in my design, as the form of the four receptacles for the oysters may be varied.

Having thus described my invention, what I claim, and desire to secure by Letters Patent, is—

The design for a dish or plate having a handle surrounded by a series of receptacles representing half-shells of oysters, as herein shown and described.

JNO. W. BOTELER.

Witnesses:
Jos. T. K. PLANT.
S. J. SHANKS.

Design Patent 7491 First Oyster Plate Design

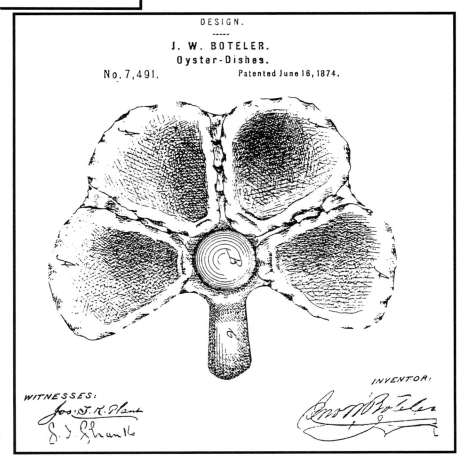

DESIGN.

J. W. BOTELER.
Oyster-Dishes.

No. 7,491.   Patented June 16, 1874.

WITNESSES: INVENTOR:

Picture of 7491 Oyster Plate Design

UNITED STATES PATENT OFFICE.

JOHN BRYCE, OF PITTSBURG, PENNSYLVANIA.

DESIGN FOR GLASSWARE.

Specification forming part of Design No. 7,948, dated December 22, 1874; application filed December 16, 1874.
[Term of Patent 3½ years.]

To all whom it may concern:

Be it known that I, JOHN BRYCE, of Pittsburg, in the county of Allegheny and State of Pennsylvania, have invented certain Improvements in Designs for Glassware, of which the following is a specification:

The nature of my improved design for ornamenting glassware, such as bowls, tureens, dishes, plates, saucers, and other similar articles designed for table and other purposes, is fully represented in the accompanying drawings.

A B represent a series of arcs struck alternately in opposite directions from springing points arranged at uniform distances in a circle around the bottom or body of the dish or vessel, the converging arcs meeting each other at their terminations, the whole forming a series of double equilateral arches, C D, around the under surface or body of the dish. The arcs are formed of parallel raised beads, cast, stamped, or otherwise produced, the crowns of the arches C D being formed at the junctures of the arcs A B, and the crowns of the arches D at the intersections of the arcs B. These lines, in crossing each other at their intersections, form polygonal or square figures G. The spaces under the arches D D are ornamented by fan-shaped figures E E, and the spaces between the upper parts of the arches C C by similar figures, F F. These spaces are formed by round or angular raised beads, crossing each other at proper angles. Under the upper parts of the arches C C are formed a series of square or diamond-shaped ornaments, alternately plain or beaded, as shown. The whole design, as above described, is formed upon the glass in raised figures or ribs by casting, cutting, blowing, or pressing, in the ordinary manner, well known to workers in glass. Around the center of the dish or other article, on the under side, is a raised angular rib, K, serving as an ornamental border for the center piece L, and also as a base for the dish to rest upon. The center piece L consists of a series of raised lancet-shaped ribs radiating from the central point of the annular rib K, and extending outward to the same. At the edge or periphery of the dish is a rounded angular or other shaped bead, M, forming an ornamental border for the dish, which serves additionally to increase its strength.

My improved design is intended particularly for ornamenting articles of glassware for table use, such as bowls, tureens, dishes, plates, saucers, salt-cellars, and other similar articles, adding highly to the beauty and finish of the same.

What I claim is—

1. The design for an article of glassware having the arcs A B struck alternately in opposite directions from a series of springing points formed at uniform distances in a circle around the body of the article, the whole forming a series of double equilateral arches, substantially as shown and described.

2. The design for fan-shaped figures under the arches D, and between the arches C, as shown and described.

3. The design for alternate beaded and plain square or diamond-shaped figures arranged within the space between the upper parts of the arcs C and the arcs D, as shown and described.

4. The design for the center piece, formed of radiating lancet-shaped projections within the annular bead K, as shown and described.

5. The design for the double arches, fan-shaped and alternate square and beaded ornaments, and radiating center piece, and projecting border, as shown and described.

6. The design for the rounded or angular-shaped ribs, forming, at their crossing, square or polygonal-shaped figures in the spaces under the crown of the arches C C, as shown and described.

7. The design for the square or polygonal-shaped figures at the intersections of the arcs A B, as shown and described.

In testimony that I claim the foregoing I have hereunto set my hand.

JOHN BRYCE.

Witnesses:
JOHN S. CAMPBELL,
D. K. BRYCE.

Design Patent 7948 Oyster Plate Design

UNITED STATES PATENT OFFICE.

THOMAS C. SMITH, OF BROOKLYN, NEW YORK.

DESIGN FOR OYSTER-PLATE.

Specification forming part of Design No. 11,009, dated February 4, 1879; application filed December 24, 1878.
[Term of patent 14 years.]

To all whom it may concern:

Be it known that I, THOMAS C. SMITH, of Brooklyn, in the county of Kings and State of New York, have originated a Design for an Oyster-Plate, of which the following is a full, clear, and exact description, reference being had to the accompanying photographic illustration, making part of this specification.

It is a plate showing an outside rim and a small concave dish in the center of the plate. Other parts of the plate are covered by a representation of sea-weed and sea-shells supporting natural oyster-shells, the whole forming the appearance of a plate containing a layer of sea-weed, on which are placed oyster-shells, and a small dish in the center.

My design represents truthfully-modeled sea-weed, oyster-shells, and small dish placed loosely upon an ordinary plate.

What I claim as my invention, is—

A design for an oyster-plate, representing a plate on which are placed sea-weed, oyster-shells, and a small dish, substantially as shown and herein described.

THOS. C. SMITH.

Witnesses:
W. E. BALCH,
H. W. KALT.

Design Patent 11009

On December 22, 1874, John Bryce of Pittsburgh, Pennsylvania was granted a design patent, number 7948, for an article of glassware. In it, areas were struck alternately in opposite directions from springing points, at uniform distances around the body forming a series of double equilateral arches.

T.C. Smith was granted a design patent, number 11009, for an oyster plate on February 4, 1879. The application calls for a plate with an outside rim and a concave dish in the center and a design of seaweed and seashells supporting natural oystershell. This design was used for the round oyster plate by the Union Porcelain Works.

DESIGN.

T. C. SMITH.
Oyster-Plate.

No. 11,009.   Patented Feb. 4, 1879.

Oyster Plate Design 11009

T. C. Smith was granted another design patent, number 12105, for an oyster plate on January 4, 1881. This was a "Design for an Oyster Plate, of which the following is a full, clear, and exact description. A plate in the form of half a clam-shell has an internal concave side with representations of natural oyster shells". It looked like a clam-shell containing a layer of seaweed and oyster shells, shellfish and small shells. This design was used by the Union Porcelain Works for their clam shell shaped plates.

UNITED STATES PATENT OFFICE.

THOMAS C. SMITH, OF BROOKLYN, NEW YORK.

DESIGN FOR AN OYSTER-PLATE.

SPECIFICATION forming part of Design No. 12,105, dated January 4, 1881.

Application filed November 22, 1880. Term of patent 14 years.

To all whom it may concern:

Be it known that I, THOMAS C. SMITH, of Brooklyn, in the county of Kings and State of New York, have originated a Design for an Oyster-Plate, of which the following is a full, clear, and exact description, reference being had to the accompanying photographic illustration, making part of this specification.

It is a plate in the form of half a clam-shell, upon the internal concave side of which is placed a representation of sea-weed, shell-fish, and sea-shells, supporting a representation of natural oyster-shells, the whole forming the appearance of a clam-shell containing a layer of sea-weed on which are placed oyster-shells, shell-fish, and small shells.

Although a clam-shell is here shown, my invention may be applied to any other shell.

The difference between my invention and other similar designs now in use is, while others represent shells modeled in conventional form and attached together without meaning, except in the instance of design patent granted me February 4, 1879, No. 11,009, wherein shells are shown on a circular plate, my design represents truthfully-modeled sea-weed, oyster-shells, shell-fish, and sea-shells placed upon the internal side of half a clam-shell.

What I claim as my invention is—

A design for an oyster-plate, representing a clam-shell, in combination with a representation of sea-weed, sea-shells, shell-fish, and oyster-shells placed upon the clam-shell, substantially as shown and herein described.

THOS. C. SMITH.

Witnesses:
W. E. BALCH,
H. W. KALT.

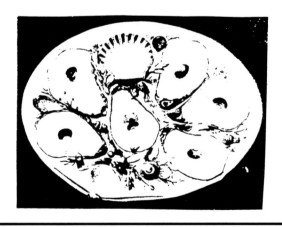

Design Patent 12105

On August 18, 1885, Edwin Haviland of Plainfield, New Jersey, was granted a design patent, number 16204, for an oyster plate design. The plate is of square outline, is concave, and its edges are its highest points. The forms of oyster-shells (generally five, although other numbers were used) have irregular ribs radiating between them in low relief resembling sea-weed.

On January 10, 1893, Theodore Haviland of Ambazac, France was granted a design patent, number 22117. "The leading feature of my design consists in a plate of shallow form, concaved and provided with a series of irregular shell like projections rising from the concaved interior, the projections at the center of the dish being more elevated than the periphery. Each of these series of several projections and elevations is in the similitude of a conventionalized sea plant or sea fern with the filaments passing out from a main vein or stem." This plate appears to have been made by the Haviland, Limoges, France manufacturer.

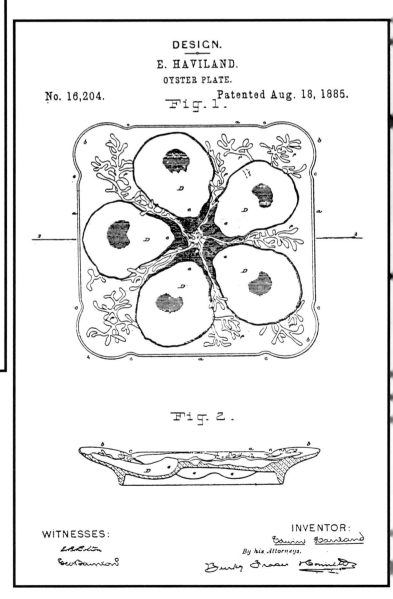

DESIGN.

E. HAVILAND.

OYSTER PLATE.

No. 16,204.   Patented Aug. 18, 1885.

Fig. 1.

Fig. 2.

WITNESSES:

INVENTOR:
Edwin Haviland
By his Attorneys.

Oyster Plate Design 16204

UNITED STATES PATENT OFFICE.

THEODORE HAVILAND, OF AMBAZAC, FRANCE.

DESIGN FOR A DISH.

SPECIFICATION forming part of Design No. 22,117, dated January 10, 1893.

Application filed October 11, 1892. Serial No. 448,584. Term of patent 14 years.

To all whom it may concern:

Be it known that I, THEODORE HAVILAND, a citizen of the United States, residing at Ambazac, in the Department of the Haute-Vienne and Republic of France, have invented and produced a new and original Design for Oyster-Plates; and I do hereby declare the following to be a full, clear, and exact description of the same, reference being had to the accompanying drawings, forming a part thereof.

Figure 1. is a plan and Fig. 2. a cross section showing the design.

The leading feature of my design consists in a plate of shallow form, concaved and provided with a series of irregular shell like projections rising from the concaved interior, the projections at the center of the dish being more elevated than toward the periphery.

In the drawings B represents the highest projections; C. the outer elevations passing into the periphery.

A. represents the irregular spaces of the dish between the several projections and elevations. Each of these series of projections and elevations is in the similitude of a conventionalized sea plant or sea fern with the filaments passing out from a main vein or stem. The design shows five of the said conventionalized ferns. The filaments have a general direction toward the deepest portion of the dish.

What I claim is.

The design for a dish substantially as herein shown and described.—

In testimony whereof I affix my signature in presence of two witnesses.

THEODORE HAVILAND. [L. S.]

Witnesses:
OR. LAMBERT,
AUGUSTE JAUHANNAM.

Design Patent 22117

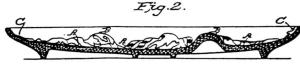

Oyster Plate Design 22117

UNITED STATES PATENT OFFICE.

EDWIN HAVILAND, OF PLAINFIELD, NEW JERSEY.

DESIGN FOR AN OYSTER-PLATE.

SPECIFICATION forming part of Design No. 16,204, dated August 18, 1885.

Application filed September 12, 1884. Term of patent 7 years.

To all whom it may concern:

Be it known that I, EDWIN HAVILAND, a citizen of the United States, residing at Plainfield, in the county of Union and State of New Jersey, have invented and produced a new and original Design for Oyster-Plates, of which the following is a specification.

In the accompanying drawings, Figure 1 is a plan of an oyster-plate embodying my design, and Fig. 2 is a transverse section thereof on the line 2 2 in Fig. 1.

I will describe my design by describing the plate embodying it with reference to the drawings, and the essential features of my design will then be defined in the claim.

The plate is of square outline, and is concave, its edges being its highest portion. The four side lines, *a a*, are straight, or nearly so, and between them are rounded corners *b b*, which are approximately semicircular, and join the side lines by slight indentations *c c*. Within the outline the concave surface of the plate is fashioned in the form of oyster-shells D D, of which the particular plate here shown has five, although other numbers may be used, and they are arranged with their apexes turned toward the center of the plate. The edges of these shells stand up in some relief above the general surface of the plate between the shells, and the deeply-concaved portions *e e* of the shells are formed by a suitable depression, as clearly shown at *e* in Fig. 2. Between the shells the plate has various irregular ribs *f f* in low relief, designed to resemble sea-weed, and this sea-weed pattern radiates from the

center of the plate outward between and apparently beneath the shells.

I am well aware that oyster-plates have been made having a design consisting of radiating oyster-shells, the outline of the plate following the irregular outline of the shells, and also that circular plates have been made with a generally concave surface in imitation of oyster-shells embedded in the plate; and I make no claim to these designs. The chief characteristic features of my design I believe to be the square plate having a concave surface fashioned into the semblance of oyster-shells. The rounded corners joining the straight sides by indentations also contribute to the effect.

What I claim, and desire to secure by patent, is as follows:

The design for an oyster-plate herein shown and described, the same consisting of a square outline with rounded corners joining the straight sides through indentations, a concave upper surface, and a series of five configurations in the semblance of oyster-shells disposed within said square outline, as shown, with their apexes toward the center and interrupting said concave surface.

In witness whereof I have hereunto signed my name in the presence of two subscribing witnesses.

EDWIN HAVILAND.

Witnesses:
ARTHUR C. FRASER.
GEO. BAINTON.

Design Patent 16204

On November 28, 1899, Frank E. Burley of Chicago, Illinois, was granted a design patent, number 31886, for an oyster plate described "as a new and original design." It had an annular rim extending down at a pronounced angle to the main body.

Design Patent 31886

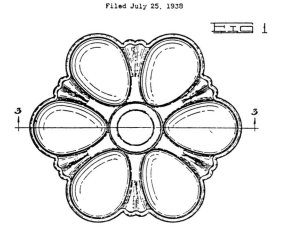

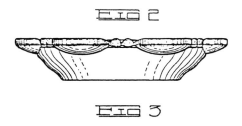

Oyster Plate Design 111504

Oyster Plate Design 31886

Arthur J. Bennett, on September 27, 1938, was granted design patent number 111504 for an oyster serving plate which he called "a new, original and ornamental design for an oyster server plate or similar article."

Design Patent 111504

Albert W. Dixon, of Sarasota, Florida, was granted design patent number 113836 on December 30, 1938 for an oyster platter holding twelve oysters.

UNITED STATES PATENT OFFICE

113,836

DESIGN FOR AN OYSTER PLATE

Albert W. Dixon, Sarasota, Fla.

Application December 30, 1938, Serial No. 82,086

Term of patent 3½ years

To all whom it may concern:

Be it known that I, Albert W. Dixon, a citizen of the United States, residing at Sarasota, in the county of Sarasota and State of Florida, have invented a new, original, and ornamental Design for an Oyster Plate, of which the following is a specification, reference being had to the accompanying drawing, forming part thereof.

Figure 1 is a top plan view of an oyster plate, showing my design.

Figure 2 is a side elevational view.

Figure 3 is a sectional view taken on the line 3—3 of Figure 1.

I claim:

The ornamental design for an oyster plate, as shown.

ALBERT W. DIXON.

Design Patent 113836

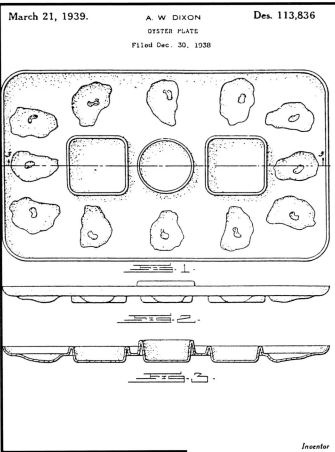

March 21, 1939. A. W. DIXON Des. 113,836

OYSTER PLATE

Filed Dec. 30, 1938

FIG. 1.

FIG. 2.

FIG. 3.

Inventor
ALBERT W. DIXON,

Attorneys

Oyster Plate Design 113836

On June 27, 1939, Irving J. Heath was granted design patent number 115398 for an oyster dish or similar article different than seen before.

June 27, 1939. I. J. HEATH Des. 115,393

OYSTER DISH OR SIMILAR ARTICLE

Filed Jan. 27, 1939

Fig. 1

Fig. 2

INVENTOR.
IRVING J. HEATH

ATTORNEY.

UNITED STATES PATENT OFFICE

115,398

DESIGN FOR AN OYSTER DISH OR SIMILAR ARTICLE

Irving J. Heath, New York, N. Y.

Application January 27, 1939, Serial No. 82,629

Term of patent 14 years

To all whom it may concern:

Be it known that I, Irving J. Heath, a citizen of the United States, residing at New York, in the county of New York, in the State of New York, have invented a new, original, and ornamental Design for an Oyster Dish or Similar Article, of which the following is a specification, reference being had to the accompanying drawing, forming a part thereof.

Figure 1 is a top plan view of an oyster dish or similar article, showing my design; Figure 2 is a side view of the same.

I claim:

The ornamental design for an oyster dish or similar article, as shown.

IRVING J. HEATH.

Oyster Plate Design 115398

Design Patent 115398

On December 29, 1942, James M. Fenton of Trenton, New Jersey was granted design patent number 134659 for an oyster dish which he called "a new, original, and ornamental Design for an Oyster Dish."

UNITED STATES PATENT OFFICE

134,659

DESIGN FOR AN OYSTER DISH

James M. Fenton, Trenton, N. J.

Application October 30, 1942, Serial No. 108,646

Term of patent 7 years

To all whom it may concern:

Be it known that I, James M. Fenton, a citizen of the United States, residing at Trenton, in the county of Mercer and State of New Jersey, have invented a new, original, and ornamental Design for an Oyster Dish, of which the following is a specification, reference being had to the accompanying drawing, forming part thereof.

Figure 1 is a top plan view of an oyster dish, showing my new design.

Figure 2 is a side elevational view thereof.

Figure 3 is a sectional view taken on line 3—3 of Figure 1.

I claim:

The ornamental design for an oyster dish, as shown.

JAMES M. FENTON.

Design Patent 134659

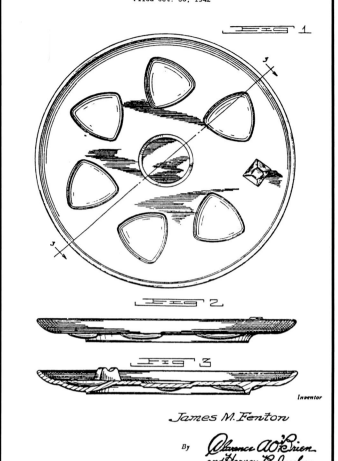

Oyster Plate Design 134659

Traditional Oyster Recipes

Oyster Soup

2 pints standard oysters with liquor
6 tablespoons margarine
4 tablespoons flour
1/2 cup thinly sliced green onion tops
3 tablespoons finely chopped fresh parsley
1 teaspoon salt
1/2 teaspoon freshly ground white pepper

Strain oyster liquor into a medium saucepan. Chop oysters coarsely. Heat liquor over medium heat, add chopped oysters and simmer for 5 minutes. Remove oysters and reserve. Add hot water to the liquor to make 5 cups.

Melt margarine in large saucepan over medium heat. Add flour gradually, stirring constantly until smooth. Gradually add the hot liquid, whisking constantly, and cook until smooth. Add onions, parsley, salt and pepper. Simmer for 15 minutes. Add reserved oysters and heat thoroughly. Serve immediately. (From *Mariner's Menu* University of North Carolina Sea Grant College. Nov./Dec. 1991)

Hooper's Island Oyster Puffs

1 pt oysters
1/2 cup Pancake Flour
1 tsp Baking Powder
Salt and Pepper
1/2 cup flour

Mix dry ingredients. Add oyster liquor. If too thick, add milk until batter is medium thickness. Dip oysters individually in batter until completely coated. Fry in deep fat until golden brown. (Anonymous Hooper's Island, Maryland Recipe)

Oyster Fritters

1 pt seaside oysters
1/4 tsp baking powder
3/4 cup evaporated milk
pepper to taste
1 cup pancake mix
1 cup Crisco

Drain oysters. Place milk, pancake mix, baking powder and pepper in a bowl. Mix and add oysters. Heat Crisco in a large skillet. Gently drop a tablespoon of batter containing two oysters into hot Crisco. Cook until brown and turn. Drain on absorbent paper. Do not add salt to seaside oysters. (Mary Mills Marshall, Saxis, VA)

Oysters, Chesapeake Style

Dry oysters on a towel, Sautee in butter, sprinkle flour over them, sautee until brown, season with salt and pepper, then cook one slice of bacon, put on top, then put brown gravy around same on platter. Dining Car Service, B. & O. RR. (From *Eat, Drink, and be Merry in Maryland*, 1932)

Oysters in Chafing Dish

2 dozen select oysters
two stalks celery
1/4 pound butter
1/2 teasp. salt
1/4 teasp. black pepper

Cut celery about half inch long, place in chafing dish, cover with water and cook. Place oysters on celery, add butter, salt and pepper, cook until edges of oysters begin to curl. Serves 3. Hotel Rennert, Baltimore. (From *Eat, Drink and be Merry in Maryland*, 1932)

French Toast with Oysters

36 oysters
1/2 teasp. pepper
1 egg slightly beaten
3 Tablespoons Fat
1 cup milk
1-1/2 teasp. salt
4 Tablespoons flour
2 teasp. minced parsley
1 cup thin cream
8 slices toast

Add milk gradually to egg, stirring constantly. Dip bread in this mixture and sautee to a golden brown. Drain oysters from their liquor and place in sauce pan with butter. When thoroughly heated, add flour gradually while stirring. Last, add cream a little at a time, and stir until smooth and well blended. Add salt pepper and parsley. Pour over toast and serve hot. Serves 8. (From *Fish and Sea Food Recipes*, U.S. Fisheries, Assoc., 1927)

Baltimore Oyster Pie

2 qts. small oysters, drained
1 cup bread crumbs
grated nutmeg or mace
1 cup butter cayenne and black pepper
Rich Pastry to line a deep baking dish
pastry for strips across the top

Line the baking dish with pastry; crimp the edge into a standing and fluted rim. Season the oysters with spices, mix in the crumbs and butter spooned into small dabs. Pour the mixture into the baking dish. Arrange pastry strips across the top. Bake this in a hot oven (450 degrees) 35 to 40 minutes, or until the crust is delicately browned. Serves 12 to 16. (From *Fifty Years in a Maryland Kitchen*, 1944)

Bibliography

Bagdade, Susan D., & Allen D., *Warmans English & Continental Pottery & Porcelain*, Radnor, PA, Warman Publishing Co., Wallace-Homestead Book Co., 1987.

Bolitho, Hector, editor, *The Glorious Oyster* New York, Horizon Press, 1961.

Brooks, William K., *The Oyster,* Johns Hopkins Press, 1891.

Centerville, MD, Tidewater Publishers, 1986.

Chowning, Larry, *Harvesting the Chesapeake,* Centerville, MD, Tidewater Publishing, 1990.

Clark, Eleanor, *The Oysters of Locmariaquer,* New York, Pantheon Books, 1959.

Gaston, Mary Frank, *The Collectors Encyclopedia of Limoges Porcelain,* Paducah, KY, Collector Books, 1992.

Hedeen, Robert, *The Oyster,* Centerville, MD, Tidewater Publishers, 1986.

Howard, Mrs. B.C., revised by Brobeck, Florence, *Fifty Years in a Maryland Kitchen,* New York, M. Barrows & Co., 1944.

Johnson, Paula, editor,*Working the Water,* Charlottsville, VA, University of Virginia Press, 1988.

Karmasan, Marilyn G, with Joan B. Stacke, *Majolica —A Complete History and Illustrated Survey,* New York, Harry N. Abrams Sons, Inc., 1989.

Klapthor, Margaret Brown, *Official White House China,* Washington, D. C., Smithsonian Institution Press, 1975.

Kochiss, John, *Oystering from New York to Boston,* Wesleyan Univ. Press, 1974.

Kovel, Ralph & Terry, *Kovels' "New Dictionary of Marks"* New York, Crown Publishers, 1986.

Lehner, Lois, *Lehner's Encyclopedia of U.S. Marks on Pottery & Porcelain,* Paducah, KY, Collector Books, 1988.

Parks, Fred, *Oysterhouse Cookbook,* Allentown, PA, 1985.

Robinson, Robert, *The Illustrious Oyster Illustrated,* Georgetown, DE, Sussex Prints, 1983.

Schneider, Mike, *Majolica,,* West Chester, PA, Schiffer Publishing,Ltd., 1990.

Stieff, Frederick Philip, *Eat, Drink and be Merry in Maryland,* New York, G. P. Putnam' Sons, 1932.

Turner, Noel D., *American Silver Flatware, 1839-1910,* A.S.Barnes & Co., 1972

United States Fisheries Assoc., *Fish and Sea Food Recipes,* New York, 1927.

Williams, Lonnie and Warner, Karen, *Oysters, Connoisseur's Guide and Cookbook,* San Francisco, CA, 101 Productions, 1987.

Index

McColla's Oyster House, Harrisburg, PA*
Historical Society of Dauphin County Harrisburg, PA